DEAD DRUNK FOR TWOPENCE

DEAD DRUNK
FOR TWOPENCE

THE PUBLIC HOUSES OF
CASTLE CARY AND ANSFORD

by

CHRIS HICKS

THE LIVING HISTORY GROUP

2016

Printed by Direct Offset, Glastonbury

printing@directoffset.co.uk 01458 831417

ISBN 978-1-902247-07-6

CONTENTS

FOREWORD

This book lists all the inns, public houses and beersellers that are known to have existed in Castle Cary and Ansford or for which I can find documentary references. The primary sources have been original documents, local directories, various books on local history and other related studies. *The Castle Cary Visitor,* published monthly between 1896 and 1915, has been a mine of additional information, particularly for the more anecdotal stories. However it should be noted that some of the articles in this magazine are occasionally contradictory and as many of the stories were often from people's memories, they are not necessarily always reliable.

This book covers the period from the seventeenth century onwards. There would undoubtedly have been inns and alehouses in the town well before this date and it remains for further research to find these and to determine which of the listed establishments were active before the earliest dates found. I have tried to indicate when and where the pubs operated and list the publicans or licensees whose names are known with any dates that I have been able to establish. Some may have been here earlier or later than shown. Often the addresses given in the books consulted are very vague, thus the locations of some establishments are unknown or conjectural. Names are often spelt inconsistently so I have tried to use the earliest version where possible.

The illustrations gathered from various collections hopefully give a feel for the look of some of the buildings. Readers seeking further pictures of the town are referred to the various books of local history listed in the bibliography, particularly those published by the Living History Group.

For some of the pubs the names of the publicans remain the only details that can be found. If the book contained only this information it might be useful but not particularly interesting. Fortunately in many cases it has been possible to add to the background and tales of some of these people and the buildings they occupied. The introduction attempts to set the local public houses in the wider historical context both nationally and in Somerset, while the notes at the end provide further details of the people and events mentioned in passing that have impinged on the life of the town over the last four centuries.

ACKNOWLEDGMENTS

It is inevitable that a book of this nature relies heavily on the help those who possess local knowledge, experts in various fields and the kindness of friends. It would be impossible to name all those who have added information and advice but the following deserve special mention for their help:

My colleagues on the Castle Cary and Ansford Living History Group including the late Ray Boyer, David Reid, Lynn Emslie, Brian Lush, Joss Mullinger and particularly Valerie Nicholls and Adrian Pearse for their extensive local knowledge. The chairman of Castle Cary Museum, Ann Brittain, and colleagues on the Museum Committee who have allowed me unrestricted access to the Museum library and archives. Anne Crawford for her historical knowledge and insights. Jenny Alderson for generous help with the Diary of Parson Woodforde and the Parson Woodforde Society Journals. Local residents Norman Legg, Will Vaughan, and Pek Peppin for additional information and guidance. The staff at the Somerset Heritage Centre in Taunton for their patience with my many queries, especially when I could not fathom out the shelf locations! Librarians in many of the libraries in Somerset where I have sought additional material. My wife Karen deserves special mention for her forbearance when I became totally absorbed and, in a clear case of 'if you can't beat them – join them,' for her time and effort in searching the local censuses and other documents for any relevant entries.

At the end of the day however the final responsibility is mine and particularly any errors or mistaken conclusions. I could undoubtedly have continued to search for further material but the line must be drawn somewhere. At this point I can do no better than quote from Revd H E Salter, the Oxford historian, who wrote:

'This book is published, not because it is finished, but because delay is unwise. Those who have long past middle age should print their material, if it can be of use to others, and not wait to make it more perfect. In a work of this kind there is a special temptation to delay, for there is a risk that some important manuscript is being overlooked, but risks must be taken, if there is to be progress.'

INTRODUCTION

Get drunk for a penny, dead drunk for twopence, and have clean straw for nothing.

This was the sign outside an eighteenth century drinking house which gives some indication of the nature of such places. But is this how we think of the typical public house? Are we perhaps more likely to think of the welcoming coaching inn of Christmas cards; the Victorian back street boozer with its etched glass windows; the ubiquitous 'Brewers Tudor' of suburbia; or the present day gastro pub? In fact pubs have been all of these things and many more besides. Over the years there have been inns, taverns, alehouses, dram shops, gin palaces, tippling shops and beerhouses. Each one had its own distinct function and identity but these differences have become blurred over time. Inns by definition provided accommodation, food and change of horses for travellers. In addition there were also taverns, which sold wine, and alehouses which, as the name suggests, sold only ale.

Beer, brewed with addition of hops which acted as a preservative and produced a better tasting product, was introduced from Flanders at the end of the fourteenth century. For about a century after that beer brewing remained in the hands of foreigners. Beer took a long time to supplant ale and was regarded as an inferior drink for many years, so much so that attempts were made to ban it. Hops were regarded with suspicion, Puritan pamphleteer Phillip Stubbes describing them as; 'a wicked and pernicious weed.' Beer was not sold in large quantities and therefore probably not in beerhouses until the late fifteenth century, when the trade was first regulated.

The brewing and selling of ale was one of the very few trades run largely by women although rarely on a large scale. Alehouses and beerhouses were often short lived, usually run by the wife who brewed and sold the drink from the front room of the house, whilst the husband was working at another occupation elsewhere. It was also extremely common, even in large establishments, for the publican to be involved in other trades or occupations.[1]

Interestingly in Somerset, for a county where cider was often the drink of choice this is very rarely mentioned. It would appear that most sources assume that it was so common as to be not worth mentioning or simply do not differentiate it from beer. This may also be because at one time there was no duty payable on cider. Early ecclesiastical records show that it was widely brewed and drunk in all periods by working men and women. In most workers houses this would have been the drink of choice in order not to use up grain that was better kept to make bread. The popularity of cider further up the social scale varied with time, partly as a matter of fashion. However, it was also consumed more widely when imported drinks such as brandy or wine were difficult to obtain because of European wars.

After the Restoration some inns and taverns began to provide better facilities and some taverns became coffee houses with the increasing popularity of this drink. Ironically, the latter were initially regarded with suspicion by politicians fearing that they might be hotbeds of radical thinking and attempts were made to close some of them. By the mid-eighteenth century the term public house appeared, while many inns became grander with the growing coaching network and the new turnpike roads. Those located alongside major highways provided the necessary change of horses for the postal service. Many became important as local social, intellectual and commercial centres and were used frequently as the venues for various events because they were often the only building with adequate space. The landlords often became major local figures, innkeeping being one of the few professions where there was the real possibility of social mobility. It became common for innkeepers to improve their standing and wealth by moving to larger and more prestigious inns. The first establishment to be called a hotel in England was built in 1768 in Exeter but the term is rare before 1800, eventually becoming more common with the advent of the railways.

The pleasures and problems of alcohol are a constant theme throughout the history of public houses. Controlling its availability was attempted as early as the seventh and eight centuries when King Ina of Wessex, King Ethelbert of Kent and later King Edgar issued edicts to either restrict the number of alehouses in each village or to legislate on the size of drinking vessels. In the late twelfth century the 'Assize of Measures' rationalised the standards for measuring liquids and grains to overcome the wide local variations that existed. In the thirteenth century the countrywide 'Assize of Bread and Ale' regulated the price of ale according to the annual price of wheat, barley or oats.

Until this period the usual sign for an alehouse was a small evergreen bush, the British variation on the Roman use of vine leaves on a tavern. Our rich heritage of inn signs has its origin in a law of 1393 which required publicans to display a sign to identify the alehouse to the ale-taster. Also known as the ale-conner this official was charged with the unpopular duty of checking the quality of ale. Some books state that he would assess this by sitting in a puddle of ale and seeing if his britches stuck to the bench. However there is no historical record or evidence for this and it is almost certainly a later invention. Many other rules were instigated over the years, indeed barely a decade goes by without some legislation aimed at the drink trade. Some form of control of drinking places began in 1495 when Henry VII gave local magistrates the power of closure. The first major act was 'The Ale House Act' of 1552 which required publicans to obtain a license.

For several centuries monasteries had provided accommodation for travellers but their suppression in the 1530s led to an increase in inns. By 1577 it is estimated that England had around 20,000 alehouses, inns and taverns of which some 2000 were inns. In Somerset at this time there were about 100 inns, 16 taverns and over 200 alehouses.

Throughout the Middle Ages only ale, beer, cider and, for those who could afford it, wine were easily available. The clientele for each was clearly defined with one sixteenth century writer stating, 'Clowns and vulgar men drink only beer and ale, but gentlemen carouse only in wine.' Brandy first appeared in the sixteenth century, originally sold by apothecaries as a medicine, and then gin in the seventeenth century.

Drunkenness had always been a problem but it became a major issue during the eighteenth century when there was a shift in drinking habits from ale and beer to spirits. The impetus for this came in 1690 when William III removed the distillers' monopoly on gin thus allowing anyone to open a distillery. With other changes in the law it is recorded in one source that by 1735 there were some five million distilleries in the country. It is unclear how this figure has been calculated and seems unrealistically high given that the best estimates for the population at the time show a total of six million people in the country. Another source states that production of gin reached eight million gallons a year at its peak but again does not give any evidence for this. A probably more reliable figure shows that in 1744 spirit licenses were issued to 23,000 premises throughout the county, roughly half of the total number of public houses at that time.

Whichever figure is the more accurate it is however clear that the result was a vast increase in supply. Gin drinking rose to epidemic proportions suggesting that a substantial proportion of the population would have been almost permanently drunk. Hogarth's famous print of Gin Lane indicates how prevalent this was. During this period drunkenness was not always regarded as unacceptable and the appalling effects that this had on the nation's health and mortality rates show very clearly in the surviving records. At one point in the 1730s the death rate was higher than the birth rate and whilst other factors may have been involved it is clear that the increase in gin drinking played a large part in this.

As the century progressed various attempts to reverse the situation were tried but with very limited success. Brewers increased the strength of beer in order to compete, then taxes on gin were increased and for a short period the cost of a retail licence reached £50, which is about £7000 in modern terms. Distillers were then restricted to wholesale only, licences had to be renewed each year and the magistrates had the power to close down undesirable houses. However, although there was some improvement in the situation after 1750 none of these measures made any significant impact on overall consumption.

In 1830 in a further attempt to change drinking habits the Budget removed all tax on beer and Parliament then passed an act 'To permit the general Sale of Beer and Cyder by Retail.' This took a different approach by allowing anyone to open a beer shop on payment of two guineas for a licence or one guinea for the sale of only cider or perry. As a result in the following year some 31,000 new licences were issued throughout the country. Added to the existing establishments this meant that by 1840 there were some 97,000 licensed premises in the country. In Somerset twenty-two parishes, which previously had one public house each, now had ninety-one beershops. In a letter social reformer Sidney Smith wrote, 'The new Beer Act has begun its operations. Everyone is drunk. Those who are not singing are sprawling. The sovereign people is in a beastly state.' The act lasted with a few modifications until 1869.

However, although beer consumption increased enormously, this act did not reduce the liking for spirits. Consumption fluctuated but the peak year for beer was 1876 when records show that some 34.4 gallons per person were drunk while in the previous year the records for spirits were also broken with 1.3 gallons drunk per head of the population. Lord Palmerston is quoted as saying that the sign over pub doors 'licensed to be drunk on the premises' now applied to the customers as well as the beer. However, from this high point until well after the First World War consumption of all drinks began to show a steady decline as the law gradually imposed further restrictions, attitudes changed and beer in particular became less of a staple component in people's diet. This last change resulted from improvements in water quality and supply. Before this time the brewing process made beer a much safer product to drink than water, and even children would be given weak ale brewed at home.

In the late nineteenth century one tenth of the occupations listed in the English census returns were those of publican, licensed victualler, inn keeper and beerseller. Large industrial cities were particularly well supplied as shown, for instance, by the famous Scotswood Road in Newcastle, some three miles long, which boasted no less than forty-three pubs. Even more rural areas supported large numbers of beerhouses and it was common practice to pay workers in agriculture and industry partly in beer or cider until this was made illegal in 1887. However as an additional perk the practice continued well into the twentieth century. Substantial amounts would be drunk, during harvest for example, each man would receive at least two quarts a day.

Not surprisingly there have always been those who were much exercised about the negative effects of alcohol and the perceived evils of public houses. Alehouses received much hostile publicity from the late sixteenth century onwards from the Puritans and also those fearing political and religious dissent. Pamphleteers saw the alehouse as an ungodly rival to church or chapel and this reflects the wider disputes in the county at the time; disputes that eventually led to civil war. Frequent attempts were made by the Church and other groups to close down as many alehouses as possible. In 1631 Somerset magistrates set about a wholesale programme of suppression and more locally in 1645 there were complaints about alehouses in North Cadbury. In 1648, under puritan Commonwealth rule, a petition was signed by over three hundred people calling for the suppression of various tippling houses, including one in Castle Cary and in the late 1650s Somerset revoked all of the existing licences, beerhouses being referred to as 'nests of Satan'. A Court Roll for the manor of Castle Cary in 1687 records fines of twelve pence each on three alehouse keepers and sixpence each on eleven brewers. None of these measures succeeded and drinking continued unabated.

Castle Cary, like most towns, has had its fair quota of inns and public houses, often more than were deemed necessary by the authorities. The argument usually offered was that there were too many drinking houses for the size of the population. However, establishing what this was prior to the advent of the census in 1801 is very difficult. The *Victoria County History* suggests that in the seventeenth century the population of Castle Cary and Ansford probably did not exceed 1500.

Historian W E Hoskins offers a method of estimating population based on analysis of the baptism registers. Combining the registers for Castle Cary and Ansford produces the following results: in the late sixteenth and early seventeenth century the population was between 500 and 600; by 1650 it was around 700 followed by a drop to under 600 until the early eighteenth century. The numbers then recover and increase through the eighteenth century reaching 1000 by 1775. How reliable these numbers are is open to question but in the absence of anything more substantive they do at least offer a usable guide. In 1801 the census gives the first reliable figure of around 1500, then 2200 by 1901 and it now stands at around 3000.

During the last three hundred years or so some fifty known drinking houses have operated in the town. There would also undoubtedly have been unlicensed premises, known in Somerset as kiddley-winks, of which at least three were reported in Castle Cary in 1758. Of the licensed premises many were very short lived and the numbers have fluctuated greatly, often from year to year. A military survey of 1686 says that there were eleven alesellers, although these are not listed in detail, plus three inns providing beds for 29 guests and stabling for 54 horses. Very few licenses were issued in the early eighteenth century but had increased to nine by 1753 despite a campaign of 1744 which attempted to close down some beerhouses.

In April of that year the vicar, churchwardens and twenty other citizens of Castle Cary placed a letter in the *Sherborne Mercury* addressed to the licensing justices petitioning them to grant only five liquor licences in the town and these only to a list of approved persons that the constable would supply. The letter went on to state that 'all others are deemed useless and more for encouraging vice and immorality.' This clearly aroused some animosity locally as in July a second letter appeared, again from the vicar and others, offering a reward for the arrest of various unknown persons who had threatened the signatories of the first letter. It begins; 'Whereas an anonimous [sic] letter was found in the Backside of Mr Seth Burge one of the Churchwardens…threatening to burn the houses, kill them or the cattle of such…endeavouring to put down some of the little Alehouses in the town or be revenged on them in some other way….' Nothing more is heard about this episode although in the following year fines for disorderly conduct were levied against the Almsford Inn and the Royal Oak both of which were fined sixpence and the Catherine Wheel which was fined three pence.

Edmund Rack in his survey compiled during the 1780s states that there were five inns in Castle Cary and two in Ansford but does not mention alesellers. He names the George and the Angel calling both 'tolerable houses.' Licences were apparently reduced to only three by the early nineteenth century and Pigot's 1831 directory shows five inns and one publican also operating as a wine and spirit merchant. The Beer Act of 1830 resulted in a sharp rise to thirteen licensed premises by 1837. The tithe apportionment books of 1838 and 1841 record five inns by name in Castle Cary and Ansford but do not specify which others are beerhouses. The numbers fluctuate slightly between 1850 and 1870 with some beerhouses changing and becoming more established as public houses and in some cases acquiring names that are now familiar.

At the Wincanton Petty Sessions in 1870 the Chairman stated that they 'got more quarrels at Castle Cary than in any other part of the district.' The following week a letter from a Castle Cary resident appeared in the local paper in which he wrote;

'Assuming this state of things to be true it becomes our duty to seek out the cause. One of the things that strikes us in the prosecution of our enquiries is that fact that there are in Castle Cary and Ansford as many drink-sellers as bakers, butchers and provision dealers put together. The one long street contains no less than nine drinking shops without including the Wheatsheaf on the way to Galhampton. There is another on the way to the station and at least four others for Ansford and Clanville. That closing some of the lowest class and most troublesome would in all probability reduce the number of quarrels and offences against the law in Castle Cary.'

When challenged on his assertion about numbers the reply showed that there were indeed fifteen drinking establishments against four bakers, three butchers and eight provision merchants.

The Temperance movement was very strong in Castle Cary with the first society being founded in 1837 and it is clear that, with the increase in beerhouses, by 1840 this had become a major issue and remained so for the next seventy years. A temperance festival in 1893 lead to the establishment of a band which made its first appearance at nearby Hadspen House. Eventually because of disagreements between the 'abstainers' and the 'moderates' the temperance label was dropped in 1897 and it became simply the Town Band.

In May 1892 a story concerning the virtues of temperance was much reported at the time. It concerned three Castle Cary boys who while walking on Lodge Hill near the town found the local shepherd's lunch with what they assumed was a bottle of beer. Two of them drank what was in fact a poisonous sheep dip, became violently ill and died shortly afterwards. The third boy survived because he stuck to his temperance beliefs and refused to take a drink.

There were three temperance hotels or coffee houses in Castle Cary in the nineteenth century. The movement's activities figure frequently in *The Castle Cary Visitor* with the editor, William Macmillan, [2] being a strong advocate. Indeed he clearly states that this and his earlier magazines were founded to support the temperance movement which becomes very apparent when examining unbound copies of the magazine where the original wrappers have survived. These carry advertisements for local businesses but it is noticeable that not one public house features among them. At the same time, because of his interest in history, Macmillan was not averse to recording memories and stories about public houses and their occupants in the magazine, something of great research value.

It is interesting to see from reading various articles in *The Castle Cary Visitor* that a number of the publicans were also very active supporters of the temperance movement. This may seem an odd stance for them to take in view of their profession but possibly, only too conscious of the effects of too much alcohol, they felt that this was a more responsible position to take. It may also have been a pragmatic approach by astute landlords in an attempt to reduce the criticism of their trade and the various attempts to close down some of the pubs

At various public meetings in Castle Cary in the late nineteenth century there were frequent calls and petitions for Sunday closing. In 1882 the population was canvassed on this issue and the result was 333 for closure and 15 against. By 1904 there were still thirteen public houses in Cary, around one for every 160 inhabitants. With the new powers available to close down public houses, the Wincanton magistrates stated that just two should be sufficient for the needs of the town! *The Castle Cary Visitor* in 1905 records following resolution passed by the Parish Council and then sent to the magistrates stating;

'That in the opinion of this Council the number of public-houses in Castle Cary is in excess of the requirements of the parish, and that a moderate reduction in the number is desirable in the interest of the Community.'

These moves certainly led to a decrease in the number of public houses, several closing within the next few years, leaving nine by 1913, and as a result of the licensing laws, social change, and improvements in water quality, to the disappearance of beersellers. The numbers have continued to fall so that now we have only four active public houses in Castle Cary taking us back to the situation of two hundred years ago.

Frequent changes to the licensing laws during the late nineteenth and early twentieth century sought to control the production and sale of alcohol. In particular during the First World War, the liberal opening hours of 5am to 12.30am were reduced to 8am to 10pm and then further to lunchtimes and evenings only. At the same time the Defence of the Realm Act (DORA) also banned the selling of brandy or whisky in railway refreshment rooms and the practice of 'treating' another person to a drink, especially serving soldiers and sailors. These last restrictions were revoked in 1919 but apart from some minor changes to opening hours most of the other wartime regulations remained in force for the rest of the century.

The late nineteenth century also saw the opening of many working men's clubs throughout the country. Many of these had been originally created or encouraged by the temperance movement with the intention of offering alternatives to the public house. However it soon became clear that for such places to attract custom and survive, selling alcohol had to be a part of their operation. As they were primarily non-profit making and could work on narrower margins, drink could be sold more cheaply than in the pubs which undoubtedly brought more custom. In Castle Cary several clubs existed, including two founded by the Liberal and Conservative parties. Both were originally in Woodcock Street until the Conservative Constitutional Club moved in 1911 to a purpose built clubhouse on Station Road, remaining there until economic pressures brought about its closure in 2013.

In recent years there has been much concerned discussion about the rate of closure of public houses but this is a process that began with the stricter licensing laws of the 1870s then continued throughout the twentieth century. In 1904 almost 100,000 pubs were recorded in England and Wales, but by 1950 this number had dropped to less than 74,000. During 1961 it is recorded that almost one pub a day closed. There was a slight recovery in the 1970s when consumption of alcohol rose by 40% mainly caused by the increased affluence of the population. Foreign holidays brought a taste for wine to more people and home brewing as a hobby became popular. Despite this the closure trend has continued so that by the early years of this century the number had dropped still further to 60,000. The relaxing of some licensing laws in recent years, particularly longer opening hours, has not led to any reversal of this trend, indeed the numbers of traditional pubs are still declining as they become increasingly uneconomic. The more stringent drink driving laws imposed in recent years have also had an effect, most particularly on village pubs. However, as licensed premises now comprise a much wider spectrum of venues, the overall number of places where alcohol is sold or consumed is in fact much larger than a century ago. Additionally drink is now available more cheaply in retail outlets such as supermarkets and people's drinking habits have changed.

There is nothing which has yet been contrived by man, by which so much happiness is produced as by a good tavern or inn.
Samuel Johnson

Public Houses were the haunts of idleness, fraud and rapine, and the seminaries of drunkenness, debauchery, extravagance and every vice incident to human nature.
Tobias Smollett

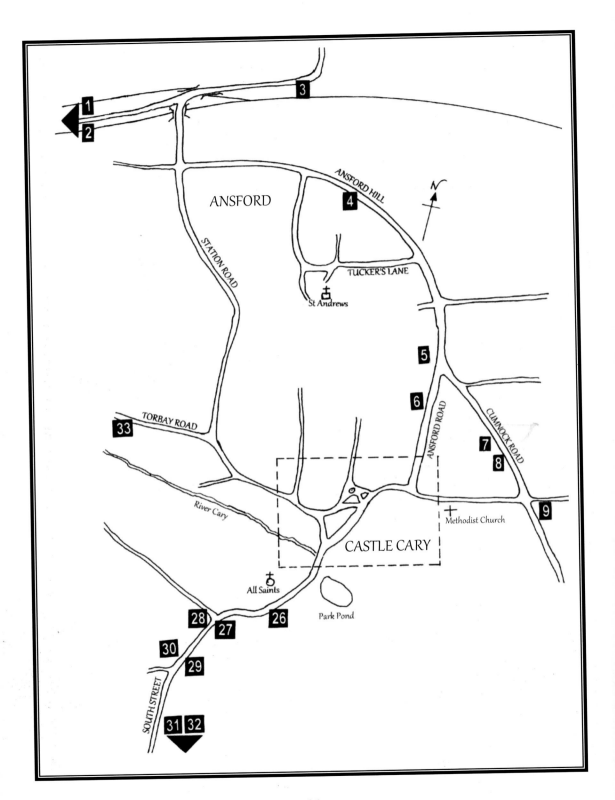

1. Royal Marine
2. Royal Oak
3. Railway Hotel
4. Half Moon
5. Ansford Inn
6. Eason's Beerhouse
7. Gould's Beerhouse
8. Grove's Beerhouse

9. Waggon and Horses
10. Angel
11. Northfield House Hotel
12. Fox and Hounds
13. Biggin's Brewery
14. The George
15. Percy's Beerhouse
16. Gilbey's Agency

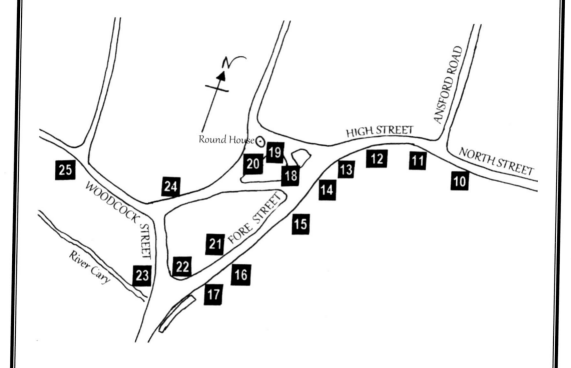

17. Phoenix
18. Catherine Wheel
19. Temperance Hotel
20. Rock of Horeb
21. White Hart
22. Rising Sun
23. Britannia
24. White Horse

25. Heart and Compass
26. Mitre
27. Golden Lion
28. Oram's Beerhouse
29. Royal Oak
30. Bay Tree
31. White Horse
32. Wheatsheaf
33. Pretty Leg

THE PUBLIC HOUSES OF CASTLE CARY & ANSFORD

Alma *see* **Bay Tree**

Angel

On the south side of Upper High Street almost opposite the junction with Ansford Road this inn occupied the buildings that are now called Wason House and Phelps House. There is possible evidence of a malthouse at the rear and in the garden there is a large cellar some 45 feet long and 15 feet wide, the function of which is unknown. It has the distinction of being the earliest named Castle Cary inn on record, being mentioned in 1620, which predates the first mention of the **George** in 1686. Wason House was built in the early 1600s and was the original inn, extended in the 1700s into Phelps House. These properties, like The George, formed part of the old castle park or estate and were bought by Anthony Ettrick around 1684. After his death, ownership passed in 1717 to John Cooper of New Sarum.

*Phelps House and Wason House
location of the original Angel Inn*

Inns have been called the Angel since the Middle Ages and reflect a connection with the religious houses that provided hostelries for travellers until the dissolution of the monasteries.[3] Like many other pubs the Angel was well known for frequent cockfighting matches and the very popular but violent games of 'sword and dagger,' 'backsword' and 'single stick'. At this time Church Vestry meetings were regularly held in the various inns around the town. In June 1779 a vestry meeting was held here at which it was agreed to proceed with the building of Castle Cary's most iconic building, the Round House lockup on Bailey Hill.[4]

The earliest recorded landlord is John Coleman who was here from 1736 until 1746 when he moved to the **George**. It is mentioned in Revd James Woodforde's[5] Diary in 1769, then in 1776 when he refers to the death of 'Jack Lucas who kept the Angel at Cary' and again in 1779 when he says that the landlord's name was Field. Edmund Rack[6] lists the Angel in his Survey of Somerset in 1781, whilst Benjamin Collier of Salisbury is recorded as the owner in 1785 with Agatha Clothier as his tenant. A deed of 1786 describes 'all that Antient Inn commonly known as Angel Inn' when it was sold to a new owner, John Burge, from the family of stocking makers of Castle Cary.

Another member of the Lucas family is recorded as the landlord in 1794 when he advertised in *The Salisbury and Winchester Journal* that the leasehold of four and a half years was for sale as he was 'tired of the business.' Clearly however he had problems other than tiredness because in the following year Woodforde records the auction of the contents of the inn as William Lucas had absconded giving the bailiffs the slip. By 1796 Mr Davis was the landlord but in that year he died in a tragic accident. The same newspaper reported. 'Last week Mr Davis of the Angel Inn, Castle Cary, on his return from Bruton was unfortunately thrown from his horse near Hadspen, and so dreadfully bruised by his foot hanging in the stirrup, that he died about four o'clock the next morning.'

The Angel closed in 1799 and the name was transferred to the **Catherine Wheel** in the Market Place. The original buildings were known as the Old Angel for a while when they became private houses. Both were gradually extended and in 1845 were purchased by the Russ family, who were connected to the Wasons of Hembridge in East Pennard. It is believed that the premises were both the residence and offices for the Russ family as attorneys. In the late nineteenth century the houses were occupied by Dr Carey Coombes[7] and Rear-Admiral Phelps.[8] Thus the two houses acquired their current names.

Ansford Inn

On the main road, now the A371, at the junction with Ansford Road. Being on the main road into Cary and near the tollhouse, this became well known as a coaching inn. There are references to a George Inn at Ansford in 1611 and again in 1619 when it was being kept by a family called Cary. *The Victoria County History* suggests that this may have been the Ansford Inn under an earlier name. In 1766 Revd James Woodforde says that the Quakers met at the inn and although this may be purely coincidental, it is recorded that a branch of the Cary family were Quakers and their houses were licenced for worship. The building is shown on the late-seventeenth century manuscript map of Castle Cary but the earliest written reference we can find to the Almsford or Ansford Inn under this name is in the Quarter Sessions records for 1711.

Then October 1723 at Taunton Assizes a Mrs Susanna Wason took an oath of allegiance to the heirs of Princess Sophia,[9] 'taken at a summons at the Ansford Inn.' That some people in Castle Cary still hankered for the return of the Jacobites is shown even as late as 1769 when *The Western Flying Post* reported a meeting at the inn;

'Forty-five of the sons of Liberty met at the Ansford Inn...drank forty-five bottles of wine, and smoked forty-five pipes of tobacco: at forty-five minutes after five the windows were illuminated with forty-five candles, and they broke up at forty-five minutes after twelve.'

The diary of Claver Morris[10] records several occasions in the 1720s when he stopped for a long lunch at the Ansford Inn to rest both himself and his horse whilst on his way to and from his home in Wells, a journey that may have taken him all day. This shows that the inn was well established by this time and by the 1730s this was the major inn in Ansford. In 1729 it is described as having 'a hall, a great parlour furnished with an oval table and upholstered chairs, a kitchen, eight bedchambers, a new cellar, a brewhouse, and a stable.'

In 1740s the hosts were James Bell and his wife Elizabeth who had previously kept the Crown Inn in Glastonbury. John Cannon[12] records in 1743 that he '...writes to Mr Bell at the inn at Ansford...' Then we have an advertisement in *The Sherborne Mercury* in 1748 where Elizabeth states that, contrary to rumour, she intends to continue as landlady at the Ansford Inn despite the death of her husband. Elizabeth Bell is best known, from her first marriage, as the mother of Reginald Tucker who in 1775 was hanged for the murder of his wife Martha.[12]

Revd James Woodforde mentions the Inn many times in his diary from the 1760s onwards as, this being his nearest inn, he often dined there or hired their post chaises to travel the area and wider afield,[13] In September 1759 he writes 'I went to the Bear baiting at Ansford Inn grounds.' By then it was an important local meeting place, hosting the County Ball, election dinners, auctions and in 1767 a masquerade ball with nine musicians, as well as providing a venue for bear baiting and cockfighting until these pastimes were abolished in the 1830s and 1840s. Cockfighting was a particularly regular attraction with substantial prizes offered and with some matches taking place over two or three days.

By the time of the murder of Martha Tucker by her husband in 1775 John Perry was the landlord and his second wife Mellior was a witness at the trial. It is not clear when they first took over the inn. It may have been in the 1750s but the first reference to them in Woodforde's diary is not until 1764 so this seems a more likely date. From then on he mentions them many times, on one occasion referring to Perry as 'a shabby scoundrel' when he failed to honour an arrangement for the use of his chaise. Much later he even refers to a newspaper report in April 1791 long after they had left the area;

'A Reward of 100 pound offered on one of the London papers for apprehending Richard Perry (eldest son of John Perry that formerly kept Ansford Inn) for running away with a Miss Clarke (about 14 years of age) from a boarding school at Bristol- her fortune great £6000 pa.' [14]

By the late 1770s the Perrys were still here, while the owner of the premises is recorded as William Stocksley who offered it for sale in 1779. The Salisbury & Winchester Journal in 1780 reported that 'Peter Buckland from Dorchester takes Ansford Inn' and in the same newspaper on 30 June 1788 it was recorded as being purchased at auction by 'F Wheeler from the Rummer Tavern in Bristol.'[15] According to an advertisement Francis Wheeler had 'furnished it in a genteel manner' and also supplied 'neat post chaises, able horses and careful drivers to any part of the kingdom.' Joseph Hillier or Hilliar was the tenant from 1789 until his death in 1799 and was followed by his widow Sarah until 1808 when she records her successor as John Bailey until he gave up the tenancy in 1815, while John Dover was then the owner. In 1804 Revd John Skinner,[16] refers to the inn twice. In October he writes, 'At Ansford Inn near Castle Cary I baited my horse for a couple of hours and got a mutton chop.'

The standing of the inn at this time may be judged from this inscription scratched on one of the windows;

To Ansford inn a traveller came,
Chill'd through his universal frame,
Into the kitchen straight he goes
First kiss'd the girl, then warm'd his nose.
The Tea was good, the Cream was sweet;
The Butter such as Gods might eat;
Full soon his blood its warmth regains,
And capers nimbly through his veins;
His horse and he refresh'd and gay;
With wonted glee resumed their way.
AW 1809

By 1824 John Perry of Hadspen was the owner. He was a cousin of the earlier Perry, whom Woodforde says had died in Glastonbury in 1791. Perry let it to Thomas Shepherd, a retired navy lieutenant, then John Coombs is recorded as the tenant in 1825-6. He went bankrupt the following year and was succeeded by William Perry who was there until at least 1832. The wording of his trade card gives a flavour of the period;

ANSFORD INN,
on the direct road from Bath and Bristol to Weymouth.
WILLIAM PERRY

returns his most sincere thanks to the Nobility, Gentry, and the Public in general for the numerous favours conferred on him since entering on the above establishment, and respectfully informs them that he has fitted it up in the most comfortable manner, and humbly solicits a continuance of their patronage and support. His horses and carriages are very superior, and the drivers may be depended upon for carefulness and civility. Well-aired beds, good Stabling and lock-up Coach Houses.

Henry Denner Blake was a well-known landlord from 1837 until his death in 1851. Richard S Blake, who was probably Henry's son, is listed as the owner briefly in 1851 and James Barnard was publican the 1851-1852, followed by Mr Simms in 1852 and Mr Groves in 1858. Now the best days of the inn were over. The advent of the railway in 1855 took away the importance of the turnpike while the building of the Market House in the same year provided an alternative venue in the centre of the town for dances and meetings; a double blow that resulted in a lingering decline for the inn.

A summary of the deeds shows that the building was owned by the Ansford rector, Revd Robert Colby, from 1872 until 1879 with James Wallin recorded as both publican and farmer from 1861 until he retired in 1876 so at that time it was still active to some extent Other notes say that Simms' widow was the last licensee and that Revd Colby caused the licence to be surrendered in 1879, at which point the coach house was converted to a cowshed. Thomas Barber, Marmaduke Morrish and Charles Chick, a shoemaker, are listed as living at the former inn in 1897, then a Major Barton in 1903. Between 1904 and 1910 occupiers included Alfred Carter and a Mr Joyce and the building was renamed Stanley House. This change is not explained nor is it clear how long this name persisted. It is still shown by this name in the directories in 1919, but even by 1911 the building was again generally known as the Old Ansford Inn. From 1925 the building was used as a furniture store for many years by Pithers, who ran a large emporium in Castle Cary, before finally being sold and restored for housing in 1951. The large porch visible in the older pictures was destroyed by an army lorry during the Second World War.

Austin, Charles

Listed as an innholder in a court roll of 30 March 1687 when he, along with two others, was fined twelve pence as a common fine for his inn.

Bay Tree

*The Bay Tree, by then called
The Alma in about 1940*

There was a public house called the **Bay Tree,** at that time virtually the last house at the far end of South Street, kept from about 1838 to 1841 by Philip Talbot, who had previously been at the **Waggon and Horses**. The 1841 Castle Cary tithe map shows him occupying what is described as a house and garden at this location and as it does not name it as an inn it was probably a beerhouse at this time. Some sources claim that this pub originated on the corner of South Cary Lane but this seems to be a case of confusion with another beerhouse.

After Talbot's death in 1841 the beerhouse closed for several years and was occupied first by James White, a blacksmith and then as two cottages by Charles Clothier and William Benjafield. In 1852 these cottages were destroyed by fire. Fires were a very common occurrence at the time and in that year there were several in South Cary, including at least two beerhouses, so it is probable that this has led to the confusion about the location.

Following rebuilding it reopened as a pub and was renamed the **Alma** from the Battle of Alma (1854) in the Crimean War. Richard Andrews, who served in the Crimea on board HMS Hermes, appears to have been the first landlord. Many Somerset men fought in the

Crimea, the Somerset Light Infantry being in action at Sevastopol, albeit very briefly when the battle was virtually over. Andrews was followed in rapid succession by John Gibbs, James Slade, James Barber and then Thomas Cook by 1857. John Holdaway was the landlord in 1860 and 1861, combining it with being both a baker and coal merchant. Thomas Cole was also there in 1861, followed by James Marshall and then by 1870 Thomas Baker, who died in 1878.

John Edwards, who subsequently retired to Torbay House, was there for many years followed possibly by his widow who later moved to Ansford Road where she lived to be one hundred. The next publican recorded is Albert Naish, succeeded by James Treasure from 1891 until 1896. Treasure then moved to Shepton Mallet where in 1902 he was charged but then acquitted of allowing drunkenness on licensed premises. In 1896 ownership of the Alma passed to the Oakhill Brewery and John White Fry[17] became the landlord until 1899 when, at the age of 29, he was found drowned in the pub well. At the subsequent inquest a verdict of suicide was returned.

Following John Fry's death the licence was transferred to his widow Mrs M J Fry, who then married Emmanuel Gibbs who was the landlord 1900-1902 followed by Charles Baker 1902-1911 and Jack Weekes in 1913. Gilbert Chappel was the licensee in the 1930s; then by 1939 the pub was taken over by his wife Fanny. She had also traded as a beerseller from South Cary House between 1923 and 1935. In the late 1950s the landlord was Leslie Southway and in 1965 Walter and Winnie Chilcott. After 1973 it was renamed the **Clarence,** then for a while in the 1980s and 1990s the **Countryman.** Recently it has reopened twice, reverting to the original name of **Bay Tree**.

Beggars Bush *see* Wheatsheaf

Biggins Brewery
William Biggin is listed as a beerseller in the High Street in 1838 and 1844. *The Castle Cary Visitor* says this beerhouse 'stood where Mr H C Pitman now lives' and then later 'where Mrs Pitman now carries on business.' Henry Pitman had a jewellery and watch shop in the premises usually known as Number 1 High Street opposite the Market House. He died tragically in 1903 after falling from a ladder whilst assisting with repairs to the clock of All Saints Church.

At some point in the late 1850s the name was changed to the **Live and Let Live.**[18] The first landlord recorded under this new name was Charles Gartell followed by John Bettey[19] who was here by 1861 but left around 1866. It continued for a few more years but closed in 1871 when the magistrates refused renewal of the license.

Bond's Hotel *see* Half Moon

Britannia

The Britannia in the 1890s

Facing the Triangle at the bottom of the town in an area always liable to flooding. The premises were built and opened shortly before 1768 on a site which has been discovered to be a former swamp. The digging of a well around 1896 showed that the original ground level was some thirteen feet below the current level. Material washed down from the hill is assumed to have raised the ground over the years. The deeds show that it was known as the Britannia from the 1790s when a troop of Yeomanry had been established in the town, despite some suggestions that it was named in 1805 when Cary raised volunteers to repel the threatened French invasion. From around 1875 it was called the **Britannia Commercial Inn** when it was the main staging post for coaches and carriers and the posting house for the railway.

James Dunford is the first known publican about 1809. His daughter married into the Andrews family who ran the pub for a large part of the nineteenth century. Three generations were named John Speed Andrews and were here from around 1819. Several members of the family served in the Royal Navy and their maritime connections were reflected in the name and decorations. At some stage the ceiling was painted with a patriotic Union Jack by Samuel Higgins a local artist, but this was later painted over and is no longer visible. An idea of the value of such businesses in this period can be gleaned from the Highway Rate Books: in 1836 the Britannia was assessed at £32 when the majority of houses were valued at just a few pounds each.

The 'middle' John Speed Andrews, who served as a purser in the Royal Navy, is also listed in the directories as a wine and spirit merchant and a maltster. He was a Freemason and masonic meetings were held in the pub. He was very much involved with local events including playing the part of Father Christmas each year in the 1840s. With others he was responsible for the building of New Road, now called Station Road, to the railway station before he retired in 1876 and moved to Tottenham where he died in 1896. One of the many Castle Cary clubs, the 'United Britons', a lodge of the Independent Order of Foresters friendly society, was founded here in 1834. In 1838 there was a Childrens' Tea Party for the coronation of Queen Victoria and the premises hosted the inaugural meeting of the Castle Cary Agricultural Society in 1852. In that same year the inn was the venue for a meeting to raise capital of £1000 to establish a company to bring gas lighting to the town.

The Britannia, like several other local pubs, issued metal tokens used for games and to buy drinks. Surviving examples have Andrews name on them, and others issued later by Charles Hallett are also recorded. [20]

In 1852 Jane Welsh Carlyle passed through Castle Cary while in a coach from Frome to Yeovil. She refers to this in a letter to her husband Thomas Carlyle, where she mentions stopping at an inn which she does not name, but is most likely to be the Britannia. She clearly was not particularly impressed as her comment was;[21] 'we stopt at Castle Carry...I grew quite frightened that I had somehow been transported to Ireland.'

Later publicans included Mr. Boon, then Thomas Lees by 1881 and Charles Hallett who combined being a publican with his butchery business from 1884 until 1902. He was followed by Samuel Herman, also a butcher, who lived at Smallway. Living originally in Galhampton, he had taken a pub in Aberystwyth before returning to Somerset, taking over the Britannia in 1902 and leaving in 1909. Three years later he sailed with his family and a young man called George Sweet on *RMS Titanic*. Samuel and George died but Mrs Herman and the two daughters survived.

Samuel Herman and his family

Henry J House from Lyme Regis became the new landlord in 1909 but by 1910 Frederick Seymour Miller, who previously worked as a horse dealer in Johannesburg, was in place. His tenure was equally short, as in the following year he went bankrupt, owing over £300 with assets of only £38. The licence was transferred temporarily to John Rapson[22] who had then recently retired as a Police Sergeant in Castle Cary. Around this time an assembly room at the Britannia was used as a roller-skating rink, a very popular pastime in this period.

Thomas Derrett was here by 1913 and stayed until 1927, followed by Frank Parsons by 1931 and Mrs A Parsons between 1935 and 1939. Later licensees include Ted Rayes and James and Eunice Martin in the 1950s, George and Gertrude Evans in the mid-1960s and S R Dunsby in 1969. Owned by Bruttons Brewery of Yeovil by the 1950s the name was changed to the **Horsepond** in 1992 when Charlie and Fiona Anderson moved here from the **White Hart**. In May 2008 the Britannia was one of several buildings in the town inundated during a violent downpour.

Cary, Francis of Almesforde

Recorded as an innholder or innkeeper in a surety of 1630 but no location is given. This man may be one of the Cary family reported to have kept the **Ansford Inn** which at this period was possibly called The George.

Catherine Wheel

On the south side of the Market Place by The Pitching and active by the early 1700s. It is mentioned by excise officer John Cannon in 1706 as the place where he accidentally encountered his supervisor 'engaged in criminal conversation' with the fourteen year old wife of another man. He mentions the inn again when referring to a public meeting there in 1738.

The next reference the author can find is not until 1774 when William Burge of the local stocking making family wrote his will in which he bequeathed to his son John a property described as; '...recently erected called or named by the sign of the Catherine Wheel.' George White was the landlord in 1775 and in his diary Revd James Woodforde mentions both White and Thomas Burge as landlords in the following year. He also mentions this inn several times in connection with his troublesome younger brother John, who was something of a rake.

The name was changed to the **Angel** when the earlier inn of this name in Upper High Street closed in 1799. In a deed of 1799-1800 it is referred to as; 'late Catherine Wheel now the Angel.' In 1800 Aaron Mogg is listed as the tenant with James Linton or Lintorn the owner.[23] No licence was issued between 1802 and 1805 and the *Castle Cary Visitor* suggests that some further rebuilding took place then. Thomas Andrews was here from 1803 until after 1806 and was probably the landlord. In 1809 the Burge family went bankrupt and the sale of their effects and property took place at the Angel in the following year.

The Catherine Wheel with the Market House on the right

In June 1814 a meeting was held at the Angel to plan a celebration for the then recently signed Treaty of Paris which had signalled a partial end to the wars with France which had lasted with short intervals since 1793. The resulting feast for all the local inhabitants was held in the Park on 23 June and most of the notables of the town were involved as carvers, tapsters and waiters. The announcement of the feast a few days earlier said;

'A dinner of Beef and Pudding will be given to the inhabitants of Castle Cary and Ansford on Thursday 23rd June inst. at 2 o'clock. Those persons intending to partake of the entertainment will assemble in the Park at the ringing of the church bell and wait until seats are assigned them; and, as it would be extremely difficult to provide those things for so large a party, each person will provide a plate, knife, fork and cup.'

By 1815 Thomas Andrews had died and in that year his widow married a maltster named Thomas White, who is listed as the owner in 1819. White was still the owner when John Coles was the tenant between 1825 and 1844, putting up a sign saying; 'bread new, cheese old, bacon good, ham cold.' 'Single-stick', a violent pastime was last played in front of the premises in about 1846, when the victor's prize was a new hat, and until 1835 a maypole was erected in the same location each year.

Coles was followed by his son, James, who then went on to the **Fox and Hounds**, followed by John Hedges 1851-1852, and James Dungey in 1855. Silas Pitman, who had previously owned the **Waggon and Horses** was also here by 1855 but he died in 1857 and was succeeded by Samuel Hayes, previously a butcher, who married Pitman's daughter Elizabeth in the same year. George Harding was here by 1859, succeeded by his widow, then R Pinney in 1861, Joseph Taylor from around 1866 to 1875, after which he moved to Bruton, and then Robert Wiggett from 1880 to 1891.

John Taylor came in 1891 but died in 1898 at the age of 39 from convulsions following sunstroke whilst on holiday in Jersey. The licence was then transferred to his widow, Julia Mary Taylor, from 1898 until 1900. She was followed by William H Farbrother 1900-1905, William Albin Biss 1905-1939 and finally Thomas Biss.[24] The licence was referred to the magistrates for review in 1905 but it remained open until 1960 and the building was then converted to shops and offices.

Centaur *see* Oram's Beerhouse

Chamberlaine, Michael
One of the few beersellers for whom we have more than just a name and a date. He is recorded as being a beerseller of Castle Cary in January 1648/9 when a petition calling for the suppression of various alehouses was presented at the Somerset Assizes Quarter Sessions. Throughout the country attempts by the authorities to close alehouses is a constant theme in records of the period. However this petition, like many others, clearly failed, as in 1657 he was still running an alehouse in the town when the quarter sessions record the following court case;

'Complaint of John Swallow the younger of Castle Cary, mason, that his game cock kept for him by Michael Chamberlyn, innkeeper, was about a fortnight since stolen; and that on Friday last Edward Murrow the elder of Almesford told Swallow that John Francis brought him a fighting cock which had already killed a cock and lost one eye besides other damage; and on seeing the said bird Swallow recognised it as his own. Depositions to the same effect by Michael Chamberlyn and Edward Murrow.'

Chappel, Fanny
Listed in directories as a beerseller at South Cary House 1923-1935. She then became the licensee of the **Bay Tree** taking over from her husband in 1939.

Clarence *see* Bay Tree

Countryman *see* Bay Tree

Cozins, Nicholas
Listed as an innholder in Castle Cary in 1630 when he goes surety for **Peter Eston**.

Crockers *see* Royal Oak

Eason's Beerhouse

Robert Eason is listed as a beerseller in 1837. One reference places him in New Road (now Station Road) but most of this road was not built until after the opening of the railway in 1856. However *The Castle Cary Visitor* states that he was 'in Ansford Lane where Henry Cooper now lives,' and the 1901 census clearly shows Cooper living in Ansford Lane (now Ansford Road)

Eston, Peter

Listed in 1630 as an innholder in Castle Cary in a surety that guarantees that he will not prepare or sell flesh in his house on days when fish is to be eaten.

Fox and Hounds

First recorded under this name in 1859, this pub is said to have succeeded a beerhouse called the **True Lover's Knot,** which was one of the buildings located in what was known as Horner's (now Pither's) Yard. For a while this yard also contained a chapel used by the Methodists from 1785 until their present church was built in 1838. Thomas Biggin is recorded here and was possibly related to William Biggin of **Biggin's Brewery**. The name of the pub is said to have been changed when huntsman Henry Honey, later the publican of the **Waggon and Horses,** killed a fox at the rear of George Horner's premises. According to the deeds most of the original buildings including this beerhouse were demolished and as a result it moved a little further up the High Street where by 1909 it sold an average of 40 barrels of beer a year.

James Coles was the landlord for many years in the 1850s and 1860s, having previously been at the **Angel** (originally called the **Catherine Wheel.)** Reuben Newport, who served in the Royal Marines during the Crimean War and was present at Balaclava and Sevastopol, was the landlord 1872-1879. He clearly did well because in 1880 he bought at auction Buttwell House and two adjoining cottages on Ansford Hill for £325. However, in September 1905 he was killed by a train near Castle Cary and at the subsequent inquest a verdict of 'temporary insanity' was returned.

29

Edward Francis was the last landlord from 1889 until 1910 when it closed, another victim of the licensing magistrates' policy of reducing the number of pubs. It became a sweet shop run by Mrs White although it retained its name for a while and is now a private house with the name Fox Cottage.

Francis, Joseph
Listed usually as a maltster from 1831 to 1837 but also operated as a beerseller. *The Castle Cary Visitor* states he lived in South Cary and suggests it was in one of cottages by then on the site of the former **Royal Oak**. He appears to have followed the family tradition as his father, another Francis, is also recorded as a maltster.

George Inn, Ansford *see* Ansford Inn

The George
Situated in probably the ideal place in the Market Square in the centre of Castle Cary, and now the longest surviving public house in the town. Various pieces of publicity that date it to the thirteenth century maybe somewhat exaggerated. Some sources date it from the 1720s, but evidence shows that it was active as an inn during the previous century. At one time the date 1673 was visible on the side of the building and one reference mentions it as being open in 1686 when it had a great chamber. Pieces of carved stonework in the external walls and in the restaurant are reputed to be fragments of the Norman castle[25] from which Castle Cary derives part of its name.

The building was part of the park or estate that extended as far as Hadspen and included the castle earthworks and manor house until it was all purchased between 1672 and 1684 by Anthony Ettrick,[26] his son William and his son-in-law William Player, barristers of Gray's Inn and Middle Temple. According to *The Victoria County History* the amount paid was £23,000, which would equate to more than £5 million in modern terms. There followed a complex series of sales and land exchanges until the whole estate was broken up. The Hoare family who built nearby Stourhead, eventually acquired Hadspen House and substantial areas of Castle Cary, including the lordship of the manor in the 1780s

Excise officer John Cannon mentions the George in 1707 when he had a violent encounter in the Market Place with an army recruiting sergeant and went to the inn to report the affray to the local magistrate. This inn, together with the **Britannia**, hosted the manor courts, a suspected thief being interrogated here in 1715. One version of the story of Jack White's Gibbet[27] says that Dick Palmer was the landlord in 1727 although there is no other record of this, the events in question actually took place in 1730, and the George had no part in them. Thomas Cox was here by 1735 and Robert Clarke in his memoirs, published in 1829, notes that Cox, who was his grandfather; 'for many years kept the George Inn at Castle Cary.' John Coleman was the landlord in 1746, having moved here from the **Angel.**

Like the Ansford Inn the George figures frequently in the diary of Revd James Woodforde. In 1773 he mentions Bill Ashford as being the landlord. He often dined and attended other events here, as in this entry for 1 March 1768, when he and his brother John went to a meeting to support a Mr Cox who was standing for election; 'We went back with him and the procession down to the George Inn, where we drank success to him and was there for an hour in the large room with the multitude.' Inns were frequently used as meeting places by election candidates, who would solicit support by handing out free beer.

The George in the early 1900s

As with the other large inns cockfighting matches were regular events, as this typical notice in the *Salisbury and Winchester Journal* in January 1784 shows;

'A Main of Cocks is to be fought at the George Inn, in Castle Cary, Somerset, between the gentlemen of Dorset and Somerset, for five guineas a battle and fifty the odd battle; to weigh, Monday, the 2nd of February, and fight the three following days.'

William Burge is believed to have been the owner of the George by 1785 with George Pew the landlord from 1785 and eventually the owner until he retired around 1809 following the death of his son, also named George, at the age of 17. The George Inn was advertised for sale in that year and was bought from Pew by Ambrose Lucas in 1811. He tried to sell in 1820 but remained here until 1822, when it was again for sale and was bought at auction by John Lapham who was the owner until 1832. Other names are recorded at this period but these are probably Lapham's tenants. First we have William Butson Chard recorded in 1825. He is still listed as here in a directory of 1831 but this may be out of date as a John Symonds is also recorded as being the licensee in 1829. He combined this job with that of a coachman and appears to have been here into the mid-1830s. Then in 1832 Lapham sold the inn to Abraham Pyke who was the owner until his death in 1842.

Most books record that during the remainder of the nineteenth century the Harrold family were tenants and then long-time owners, starting with Francis William Harrold from 1835 until 1872. However, a study of surviving deeds and other documents shows that the ownership was rather more complex. Harrold's wife Charlotte was the elder daughter of Abraham Pyke who bequeathed the George, firstly to his widow, then in three equal shares to Charlotte, her brother Alfred and her sister Mary Ann. Thus although Francis Harrold was in law entitled to his wife's share he never owned the inn in its entirety. Curiously, despite this bequest, the inn had been advertised for sale by order of Abraham Pyke's executors in *The Wincanton Journal* for 11 April 1842 described as;

'...situated in the centre of the flourishing market town of Castle Cary, comprising a bar, three front parlours, large dining room and two kitchens, with other requisite offices on the ground floor, and a sitting room and nine good bedrooms over; adjoining which is a large clubroom, good cellarage and brew-house, stabling for nearly 100 horses and lock up coach houses and yard. Two gardens and a piece of pasture adjoining.'[28]

Castle Cary Cycling Club outside the George in May 1898

The large clubroom at the back of the inn was used for various meetings and on occasion, theatrical performances by travelling players. In 1845 it had to be rebuilt after it was destroyed in a fire caused by Edward Biggin, the ostler, going into the hayloft with a candle. For many years the Post Office was located at the George and we can also see that during Francis Harrold's tenure the building was used for a variety of purposes. In 1866 the George is described in the local directory as; 'George Commercial Hotel and posting house and Inland Revenue office and auctioneer, appraisers and estate agent.'

After Francis Harrold's death in 1872 his widow, Charlotte, took over the licence. Considering the number of other occupations that her husband pursued it is likely that she had been running the inn for many years. When her brother Alfred died unmarried in 1873 he left his share to Charlotte and two years later she purchased for £100 the remaining third, by then held by the children of her sister, who had died some years earlier. Charlotte died in 1892 and left the inn to her children and grandchildren and two of her unmarried daughters, Catherine and Elizabeth Mary Harrold ran the inn from 1893 until Elizabeth, known as Bessie, died in 1903.

The George was sold to the Somerton Brewery[29] in 1904 and according to the directories William James Beer Payne was the licensee 1904-1927. Somewhat confusingly, *The Castle Cary Visitor* refers to him as Frank Payne who came from the **Railway Inn** and certainly the publican there is listed under this name. Richard B Whittington was the licensee by 1935, then R L Watts in 1937 and Laurence Allen in 1939.

In World War II a Grenadier Guards motorcycle platoon was billeted at the George during 1940. Their commander was Brian Johnston, later to become famous as a radio cricket commentator. In 1942 the inn was taken on by William Mackintosh Lumsden and his wife Hilda, while Cyril Cornish is recorded in 1957. More recently the hotel was bought by Greene King of Bury St Edmunds. In 2002, the thatched roof was severely damaged by fire during renovation work.[30]

Gilbey's Agency

This was an off-licence as part of the bakers and confectioners shop in Fore Street, run by brothers Sydney and Wosson Barrett in the late nineteenth and early twentieth centuries. Part of their premises now form the Co-op.

Having the only wine licence in the town at the time, they gained the off-licence agency to sell the wines and spirits produced by Gilbey's, a company best known for their brand of gin. They also sold Buchannan's Whisky, Dow's Port, and Ales and Stout produced by Whitbread's, Rogers', Usher's, Anglo-Bavarian and Oakhill Breweries. They are listed as holding the agency between 1883 and 1897 but they were still there in the 1920s.

Golden Lion

Chapel Yard, South Cary. In the house on the corner of Chapel Yard now called Westholme, and the adjoining property, Avenue House. In the late eighteenth or early nineteenth century John Bulgin, a carpenter, who was the copyhold tenant and later the owner, converted the premises into an inn. By 1808 it was called the Golden Lion and was occupied by Jeremiah Dean.

Bulgin sold it to Edward Dean, an innholder of Shepton Mallet, who sold it to George Hill, a tollgate keeper, in 1809. James Turner is also recorded as the landlord in 1809-1810. In turn Hill sold the building to William Stallard, a brewer, in 1813. During Stallard's ownership it ceased to be an inn because of the behaviour of the clientele. Members of nearby All Saints Church were scandalised by reports of the goings on at the Golden Lion particularly during services.

One Sunday, leaving the congregation singing a particularly long hymn, the vicar[31] appeared unannounced at the pub and finding a number of his parishioners there used his influence to have the place closed down. The property was divided, became houses and, in a real reversal of use, a Congregational Chapel, also known as the Zion Chapel, was built in the garden in 1816. The Chapel closed in 1979 and the building was converted into houses.

Gould's Beerhouse

Recorded in *The Castle Cary Visitor* as being located where 'William Winter lives in Cumnock Road.' The census returns for 1901 show this was the tenth in the row of cottages on the western side of Cumnock Road. They are also described as being 'built by Edward Gould before 1882.' It seems likely that some may have been built considerably earlier as the tithe map of 1840 clearly shows a short row of buildings here. The cottages were all demolished to make way for the row of prefabricated houses called Cumnock Crescent after the Second World War and these were in turn replaced by the houses that include Olympic Drive built 2012-13. George Gould is recorded as a beerseller in 1866 but no location is given. Probably the man who ran this beerhouse and related to the builder.

Great Western *see* Railway Hotel

Greenhill's Guest House *see* **Half Moon**

Groves Beerhouse

Recorded in the *Castle Cary Visitor* as being 'where Richard Hebditch now lives.' Like **Gould's Beerhouse** this was one of the cottages on Cumnock Road, in this case number 16 in the 1901 census but these numbers were fairly arbitrary. James Groves is recorded as being there in 1838-1840. This again shows that there were cottages here before 1882.

Half Moon

Situated on the main road near the top of Ansford Hill. It is not clear from the records when this inn opened but some of the buildings may date from around 1625. The earliest record in the *Victoria County History* is from 1742. The first published record is in December 1770 in Revd James Woodforde's Diary where he tells the following sad story;

'A poor young fellow that drove a waggon of Mr Lockyer's was about the middle of the night killed by the waggon going over him as he was going down our hill in a great hurry...The Half Moon Inn would not take the poor fellow in.'

In 1772 the freehold of the building, with 27 acres that had originally been part of the local manor, was purchased from the then owners, Benjamin and Francis Collins of New Sarum, and conveyed to Henry Martin of Bruton to be held in trust for the occupier, William Hurt. The inn is not named in the documents at this point but it is clearly the Half Moon. At some stage Hurt took over ownership and may possibly have rebuilt all or part of the premises. When he died in 1779 his brother and heir conveyed the land to William's widow, Grace. She in turn bequeathed the land to John Burge of Castle Cary who mortgaged it to Thomas Chamberlain of Evercreech for £800 and at this point it is named the Half Moon. Grace Hurt died in 1786 at the age of 84, having been at the Half Moon for over forty years. At her retirement she also had about £1500 which she distributed in amounts of £5 to £100 each to over forty people.

Then as now the newspapers were always keen to report criminal activity and we find a report from the Somerset County Assizes in Wells in August 1784 when John Horner of Castle Cary was sentenced to three years hard labour on the River Thames for stealing six holland shifts from Mrs. Grace Hurt of the Half Moon. The marriage of Henry White of the Half Moon is recorded in the newspapers in 1786. Then in 1788 Rachel Gulliver, described as a servant to Mrs Henry White of the Half Moon, was committed to Shepton Mallet gaol for stealing money from her employer's cash boxes. Renaldo Roberts is recorded here in 1814 while the death of his wife, Hester, is reported in *The Salisbury and Winchester Journal* in 1825. George Roberts, probably their son, carried on the business after this and is listed here in 1830-31, with Renaldo's death recorded in 1833. John Humphries was here from 1832 until 1844 being succeeded by a landlord named Groves and then by James Wallin both of whom were at the **Ansford Inn** at a later date.

Before the coming of the railway in the 1850s the extensive yard was used by coal carriers on their way from the Somerset coal fields to Wincanton and Yeovil. It was common to see a line of up to thirty carts between here and the Old Parsonage. The carters from the Cruse and Gass sawmill would also stop here on their return journey and whilst the men would go into the pub for a drink the horses and waggons would continue driverless down the hill and back to the Clanville sawmills.

James Pearce was here in 1850-1853 followed by Joseph Gale in 1861, Albert Higgins by 1866, John Rawlings in 1872, then Thomas Coleman, Walter Warren and Orlando Jennings by 1875.

The yard was converted to cottages before 1880. George Read was here by 1882, followed by Henry Willis 1883-1889, Thomas Higgins 1891-1894, William Joyce 1897-1914, Mrs Elizabeth Joyce 1919-1927 and their son William Eric Joyce from 1931. It remained open despite having its licence referred to the magistrates in 1905. There was said to be illegal cock-fighting in the cellars as late as the 1950s.

Owned by the Devonshire Brewery by 1951, in that year they sold the inn to Brutton, Mitchell and Toms of Yeovil. In 1957, when the licensees were Cecil and

Outside the Half Moon in the 1940s, landlord Eric Joyce at the front.

Frieda Farrant, Bruttons sold the part of premises known as Half Moon Cottage for £750. The property conveyance contains a clause requiring the new owner to brick up the connecting doorway to the inn, and another forbidding them from opening this cottage as a pub. However the inn only survived for a further six years closing in 1963 with the departure of the last licensee, Raymond Victor Wilton, who went briefly to the **Waggon & Horses.** During the 1980s part of the building was run under the names of Bond's Hotel and Greenhill's Guest House but it has all now been converted to private houses.

Ham, Matthew

Listed as an innholder in a court roll of 30 March 1687 when he, along with two others, was fined twelve pence as a common fine for his inn.

Heart and Compass

In what was then called Mill Lane, although it later became part of New Road, (now Station Road), opposite the junction with Victoria Road. It was built in 1872 by Thomas White[32] who is listed as a beerseller between 1870 and 1875 and was here until at least 1881. By that year it was known as the Heart and Compass; by the 1890s it was with the Squibb family who owned it until 1952 with John Taylor shown as the licensee in the 1891 census.

In 1899 there is a reference to 'Mrs Hill of the Heart and Compass' which suggests she was the licensee at that time. John Frederick Squibb is also recorded as the publican in 1901 and as a beerseller in Station Road between 1897 and 1914. Originally a blacksmith, in 1906 he also started a coach building business on the site which had formerly been Moody's brickyard directly across the road from the pub. The business gradually changed from coach building to a garage, closing in 1987 when the buildings were replaced by housing. Julia Squibb is also listed as a beerseller 1923-1935 but by 1939 she is the licensee of the pub. Reginald and Mabel Higgins were here by 1957 and John and Susan Blackmore in 1965. The name was changed to the **Two Swans** in 1996 but it closed in 2006 and has now been reconstructed as private houses.

Horsepond Inn *see* Britannia

Kinge, Richard
One of two winesellers recorded 'in the year Charles I came to the Throne' (1625) when he paid 10s for a licence.

Lamb and Flag
It is not certain whether this public house was actually in Cary or in one of the surrounding villages. The only record is an article in the *Proceedings of the Somerset Archaeological Society* describing a trade token of 1660 which bears on the obverse 'Wm Ireland – The Lamb & Flag' and on the reverse 'In Carey Land 1660 WKI.' Caryland is a somewhat loosely defined term that is used to describe the area around Castle Cary and the course of the River Cary as it flows onto the Somerset Levels. The Lamb and Flag is often a reference to the Knights Templars.

Live and Let Live *see* Biggins's Brewery

Mitre
Situated in Park Street opposite All Saints Church, according to *The Castle Cary Visitor* it was known popularly as "Knacker's Hole." In her recollections, in *Memories of Castle Cary and Ansford*, Winnie Chilcott says that this was the name of an 'awful old tenement' that was next to the Mitre, which seems like a pretty accurate description of the building as in 1841 it is described as comprising fifteen tenements. However the deeds of nearby Cleve Cottage clearly show that for many years this house was also known as Knacker's Hole. The deeds also show that this property, various other nearby buildings and the adjacent land were once under single ownership and may indeed have been a horse knacker's yard. *The Castle Cary Visitor* says that a market for worn-out horses was held in this area and that Cleve Cottage was occupied by a horse dealer. Thus the name became used for the area more generally and the public house in particular.

Robert Gibbons was at the Mitre before 1831 and may have built the house. Uriah Marshalsea, Gibbons' son in law, was here in 1838 and one source shows him still here in 1853. The same source says John Kemble was here in 1854, while he is also listed as a beerseller in 1840 and then in the 1841 census in Gibbons Row. This is presumably named for the builder and would appear to be the tenement described above. It is possible that there were two different beersellers here at that time, but as the evidence is inconclusive it seems most likely that this is in fact the Mitre. Then we have Thomas Marshall who is listed in one directory as here in 1861. However another directory of the same period lists George Hodges here from 1859 to 1864, followed by Thomas Brake 1864-1883 and then his widow Elizabeth 1883-1892. Henry Frederick Brake, who was probably their son, is also shown here briefly in 1892 when the pub was sold to the Sherborne Brewery for £1100. He was immediately followed by Alfred Hill 1892-1896, and then Francis Culliford 1896-1907 who was the last publican.

The Mitre with Cleve Cottage on the right

The provisions of the new licensing act in 1904 signalled the end for the Mitre, it being deemed that there were too many pubs in the town and it closed in 1907, the property then being sold for £200 to Lionel Merrick. Apart from Cleve Cottage all these buildings have now disappeared, the tenement replaced first by the Church Room and later two cottages while the pub was replaced c1960 with a block of four flats with the name Mitre Place. The large inn sign, painted on tin, is now in the care of Castle Cary Museum.

Nichol, Capt John

There is a single reference to this man in *Morris' Directory* of 1872 as being in South Cary where he is listed as 'agent for the Litre Bottle Wine Company.'

Northfield House Hotel

A hotel occupying extensive premises at the top of the High Street opposite the junction of Ansford Road. In *Kelly's Directory* of 1935 the proprietor is listed as Mrs W J B Payne, whose husband had been licensee of the **George.** In the 1950s it was run by Ralph and Laura Royle who were there until the mid-1960s and then Adrian and Margaret Morgan in the 1980s. It is now a retirement home.

Oram's Beerhouse

This beerhouse in South Cary moved after a fire and the notes about its later location are unclear. The Castle Cary tithe map of 1840 clearly shows a property on the corner of South Cary Lane which is occupied by Edward Oram and he was still there in 1851. By 1852 it was occupied by Thomas White, a greengrocer, when it was destroyed by one of the several South Cary fires of that year. There was a local belief that due to legal complications nothing was then rebuilt on this piece of land and indeed the area is still open and has not been built on.

There are slightly confusing notes in *The Castle Cary Visitor*. The first says that eventually this beerhouse was located in the house now known as Greystones in South Street, moving here in 1852 as a result of the fire. This is just south of the junction with South Cary Lane and beyond the former Mackie cheese warehouse (now called March House) that was built in 1901.

Later notes in the *Castle Cary Visitor* say that the beerhouse licence was transferred to a house 'on the site of Mrs. Litman's present house' and 'where Litman and Son are.' Litman and Son were basket makers and like many businesses in the area their adverts simply give the address as South Cary. Studies of the census returns unfortunately do not provide a more precise location for this business. Probably they were occupying the house now called Greystones. There is also a suggestion that the beerhouse may have been called the **Centaur** at some stage.

Parks's Beerhouse *see* Pretty Leg

Percy's Beerhouse

There is a single reference in *The Castle Cary Visitor* stating this was 'where Mr. Bellringer now lives.' Bernard William Bellringer was a coach builder who operated originally in South Cary, and later from a shop in Fore Street.[33] The 1840 tithe map shows this property listed as a house, shop and garden occupied by Jacob Percy. In Bragg's 1840 Directory Jacob Pursey is listed as a provision merchant and his wife as a straw bonnet maker in Fore Street. Clearly, as was often the case, beer selling was an extra trade.

In another directory a Jacob Pinsey is also listed as a beerseller but it seems likely that this surname is a misprint. Some books suggest that the building may have been a coaching inn at an earlier period but no records supporting this have been found. The building subsequently became Jack Norris' Garage and is now a hardware store.

Phillips, Thomas

A beerseller listed in the directory of 1861 but with no precise location given.

Phoenix

This inn occupied extensive premises on the eastern side of Fore Street running down to the Horse Pond. Recorded as active in 1718 and 1748 it seems to have ceased trading around 1800. In the *Western Flying Post* 22 August 1748 there is a notice stating that there; 'will be Back Sword plaid [sic] at the Phoenix Inn…in Castle Cary.' The phoenix is a reference to the arms of the Seymour family who, with the families of Lovel and Zouche, were lords of the manor of Castle Cary for nearly four centuries.

Within a few years of the inn closing the buildings were replaced by shops and houses. In 1809 some of these were purchased by John Speed Andrews who was soon to become the landlord of the Britannia. Then more buildings are detailed in a lease of 17 January 1818 which describes them as; 'dwelling-houses, gardens and premises known by the name of the Phoenix.' The lease was drawn up by William Horner on behalf of the owner, his aunt Mary Horner of Portsea in Hampshire. It is possible they may have been related to the Horners who owned Horner's Yard in the High Street, later known as Pither's Yard. The document shows that John Speed Andrews was leasing these premises for a yearly rent of £21 for the lifetime of Mary Horner.

Pretty Leg

Beerhouse in a cottage in Mill Lane (now Torbay Road) and sometimes known as **Park's Beerhouse**, from William Park who was here 1842-1853

Railway Hotel

Next to the station constructed with the building of the railway in 1856, the hotel was opened 1861 on surplus land sold by the railway company. Renamed **Great Western Hotel** in 1872 it was listed as **Railway Inn** in 1875, **Great Western Hotel** in 1901, **Railway Commercial Inn** in 1902 and **Great Western Hotel** again in 1905. John Hookey is shown as the first landlord, then his widow Mrs Sarah Hookey between 1866 and 1875, Thomas Pearce, who also traded as a coal merchant and had previously been the first policeman stationed in Castle Cary was here from 1877 until at least 1880 and then Ashley Bellinger between 1883 and 1891.

Herbert John Roles, who also produced mineral water, was the landlord from 1894 until 1897. He had previously worked for his father William, landlord of the Bell Inn in nearby Ditcheat. Later Herbert moved to another Railway Hotel, this time at Evercreech, where he died in 1905.

Robert Gibbons was the landlord from 1899 to 1901 when he died suddenly. The licence was transferred to his widow Harriet Ann Gibbons and then according to *The Castle Cary Visitor*, at the same time, temporarily to William James Beer Payne. However in 1902 the landlord here is shown as Frank Payne, and by 1904 William Payne is at **The George**. In July 1905 a dinner was held at the hotel to celebrate the opening of the new line from Castle Cary to Charlton Mackrell thus shortening the route to Taunton and further west. The landlord then was Henry George Russell but his death at the age of 48 is recorded the following month. His widow, Mrs. Frances Russell is recorded as being here until 1923, followed by Arthur Francis 1927-1931 and George Knott Phillips 1935-1939.

In 1940 the hotel was bought by Ted and Irene Wisbey who were in residence on a drizzly morning in September of 1942 when a Junkers 88 bombed the station. In the recollections of a local resident it was said that the German pilot had been at school in Bruton, knew the area and had followed the line up from the coast at Weymouth as far as Castle Cary. He dropped four bombs of which two destroyed parts of the station and killed three men. One exploded in the river Brue nearby while the fourth bounced off the road by the west wall of the hotel, passed through the building and exploded in the garden at the back. The building was damaged beyond repair, demolished and, although the Wisbeys kept the licence, never rebuilt. One story says that the local anti-aircraft battery did not respond to the attack because the officers who could give the order were in the **George** having a drink!

Ranger, Edward
A single listing of this man as a beerseller in 1861 occurs but with no specific location given. Recorded in the Castle Cary parish registers is his marriage in 1860 to Anna Marshalsea.

Ricks, William
Listed as beerseller in 1837 but no location is given.

Rising Sun

Listed sometimes as a coffee tavern and refreshment rooms, this was a local temperance hotel. It was located at the end of Fore Street when this part of the road was called Ashby Place until renamed the Triangle in 1914. It was operated by the Poole brothers who owned an aerated water business across the road adjoining the Britannia. *The Castle Cary Visitor* has several articles about its origins all giving slightly different versions. However advertisements in another magazine clarify the situation.[34] William Poole opened the Rising Sun in 1879 with his brother Thomas, who had apparently come from Bath originally to work as a coachbuilder, as the manager. William then moved to Reading and sold the coffee house to his brother in 1884. Thomas then also moved, in this case back to Bath in 1897, where he lived until his death in 1907 after his bicycle was in collision with a milk cart.

Thomas Poole's departure was reported in *The Castle Cary Visitor*; 'Mr T Poole is leaving for Bath' and; 'we are to have a new Temperance Hotel.' At this point William Herbert Brake became the landlord and is listed in the directories as such up to 1931. However even by 1906 it was being advertised simply as refreshment rooms or coffee tavern and the name Rising Sun only crops up occasionally. In 1911 this property and the adjoining buildings changed hands when they were bought for £650 by William Albin Biss the landlord of the **Angel** (formerly the **Catherine Wheel** in the Market Place. From 1931 Brake is listed as a dairyman, while in the directories of 1935 and 1937 the establishment is still listed as Brake's Temperance Hotel. In *Memories of Castle Cary and Ansford* many of the contributors recall Brake's Dairy on the Triangle and their delivery cart. It is perhaps rather ironic that the rising sun is part of the coat of arms of the Worshipful Company of Distillers! (*See also* **Temperance Hotels & Coffee Houses**)

Rock of Horeb *see* Temperance Hotels and Coffee Houses

Royal Marine

Recorded in Clanville in 1845 and 1881, possibly the same pub as the beerhouse recorded at Blackworthy in 1859 and 1861 but the precise location is unknown. Noted in *The Castle Cary Visitor* as the house of Mrs Chant, who is listed in the 1901 census as living in Clanville. Landlords recorded include Richard Andrews and John Gibb but it has not been possible to establish precisely when they were in residence.

Royal Oak

On the Somerton Road at Clanville opposite the sawmill entrance this beerhouse is recorded in 1851 and was open until 1872 or later. Samuel Pitman is recorded as a beer retailer in 1846, possibly in these premises. He was certainly the publican here in 1859 until his death in 1871, followed by Mrs Charlotte Pitman in 1872 whose own death is recorded in 1888. By 1947 it was a farmhouse that preserved the name and is now a private house. Royal Oak is a reference to Charles II who had a local connection in that he was hidden in Castle Cary, possibly in the Manor House or at a house in Ansford, during his flight after defeat at the Battle of Worcester in 1651.

Royal Oak

In South Cary on the site now occupied by a terrace of cottages including Tudor Cottage on the east side of South Street. This was apparently furnished with furniture, pewter and brewing vessels belonging to the lord of the manor in 1729. In 1745 the Royal Oak was one of the pubs fined sixpence for disorderly conduct.

Revd James Woodforde sometimes refers to the Royal Oak in his diary as 'Crockers' and in 1764 names the landlady as Mrs Croker. There is also a Jonathan Crocker[35] who is mentioned elsewhere in his diary and the editors claim he was the landlord here but the evidence suggests otherwise. One particular entry in Woodforde's diary again shows the various uses made of public houses in this period. In July 1773 he paid two shillings so that he and his niece Jenny could visit the Royal Oak to see;

'Nevil's grand machinery, being the whole of the woollen manufactory, from one end to the other, and all in motion at once. It is very curious indeed and 3000 movements at once going, composed by Mr Nevil himself and which took him 20 years in completing it.' [36]

The Royal Oak had closed by 1785 when the ballroom, opened in 1779 and used for concerts and other entertainments, was converted to a Sunday school and the rest into cottages known as the Old Royal Oak by 1810. *The Castle Cary Visitor* notes that this is one of the buildings that fell victim to a fire in 1838 on 'the site of Mr T Gifford's cottage in South Cary now occupied by Mr Potter and Mr Mogg.'

Savage Cat *see* Wheatsheaf

Shoulder of Mutton
Location unknown. Active in 1703. The name may refer to the fact that food was available as well as drink but could also indicate that the owner combined the trade of butcher with that of publican.

Slade, James
Listed as an innholder in a court roll of 30 March 1687 when he, along with two others, was fined twelve pence as a common fine for his inn.

Temperance Hotels & Coffee Houses
The Temperance movement was very active in Castle Cary, starting in 1837, undoubtedly as a reaction to the sharp increase in beerhouses since the Beer Act of 1830. Several groups were formed, mainly connected with the churches, and lasted into the twentieth century. In addition to the **Rising Sun** at the bottom of Fore Street two other establishments are recorded, both on Bailey Hill.

The first was founded in 1844 by a group of Rechabites,[37] under the name of 'The Rock of Horeb.' They met at a coffee tavern, the house of Silas Hoskins on the south side of Bailey Hill, a few doors along from the Pitching. Hoskins was in the building trade and owned a considerable number of properties in the town. He worked variously as mason, carpenter, surveyor and stamp distributor. He was also much involved in local affairs, being a parish constable for a while, and died in 1894. It is not certain how long the group lasted although it was still active in 1854. It is now difficult to determine precisely which house this was but it is likely that it was the building that is now a butcher's or possibly a room behind accessed through the corridor.[38]

The second, a Temperance Hotel at the top of the Pitching, appears to have opened in the early 1870s but had closed by the late 1880s. It is first recorded in a directory of 1875 and again in 1883 under the occupancy of George Hunt. The census of 1881 describes him as a blacksmith, and his wife Frances is listed as the landlady. By the 1891 census Hunt and his family had moved to Marston Magna.

An auction poster for May 1878 offers the building for sale describing it as; 'formerly known as the Bank but now used as the Temperance Hotel.' *The Victoria County History* says it was 'in a redundant bank and remained open until 1931 or later.' This date cannot be correct as this hotel is not in any directory after 1883 nor any other census. Further, *The Castle Cary Visitor* in 1901 says that it was long closed by this date. The magazine was a strong supporter of the Temperance movement so the fact that this article is the only reference it makes to this hotel does suggest that it was very short-lived.

In the same article *The Castle Cary Visitor* states that the hotel was located in the building on Bailey Hill at the top of the Pitching by then occupied by Mr. Woodforde. Stuckey's Bank, which originated in Somerton, may have been located here as they re-opened their branch in Castle Cary in 1856. However, another note says that this building was not erected until 1857 and in the 1861 census it is shown as unoccupied. It may be that its use as Stuckey's Bank followed before they eventually moved to the High Street.

Randolph Woodforde is recorded as a solicitor from 1875, in the High Street in 1883 but by 1889 he had moved to this building on Bailey Hill, which confirms that the hotel had closed between these last two dates. The building remained solicitors' offices under various occupants until 2011 when it became a private house.

Three Cups
In business during the Interregnum and possibly later but the location is unknown. The three cups was the badge of the Worshipful Company of Salters.

Tranter, John
One of two winesellers recorded 'in the year Charles I came to the Throne' (1625), when he paid 10s for a licence.

True Lovers Knot
This beerhouse, open in 1838 when Thomas Biggin was the landlord, and again in 1842, on the corner of Horner's Yard (later Pither's Yard.) was probably the precursor of the **Fox and Hounds.** True lovers' knots were made as love tokens and often worn as hair decoration. The use of knots as design has a long tradition particularly in embroidery and gardening.

Two Swans *see* Heart and Compass

Waggon and Horses

Located in the area known as Townsend at the junction of the A371 with Wyke Road. As this was a turnpike road the pub was probably quite long established and the buildings appear to be partly of the eighteenth century. However the earliest record found shows that in 1814 Samuel Hix was the occupier, then possibly Charles Garland, followed in 1832 by Philip Talbot, who by 1838 had moved to the **Bay Tree** in South Cary. In the Tithe Apportionment of 1838 the owner of these buildings is shown as Martha Hix, with several tenants including James Francis who is listed as a beerseller. Not named as an inn, it was clearly still a beerhouse at this date.

The next recorded publican is Silas Pitman who may have been here by 1844 when he is listed as a beerseller in Ansford. He was certainly here from 1851 to 1855 and would have been responsible for putting stabling at the front of the pub when the cottages previously there were destroyed by fire in 1850. He is also recorded in the Ansford Parish Registers as a turnpike keeper in 1852. Silas had a very smart sign over the door, the work of one George Higgins, a local artist and the son of Samuel Higgins who painted the Union Jack in the **Britannia**. George charged £10 for the sign, at which Silas complained. 'Why' said George 'what more do you want; you have a waggon and horses, a waggoner, cocks and hens, and pretty well a farmyard.' The sign was afterwards purchased by an admirer of the fine arts, so presumably Silas made a profit!

After Silas left for the **Angel** (formerly the **Catherine Wheel**) in 1855, he was followed by James Creed; then in 1861 the pub was kept by Henry Honey, the huntsman of the Blackmore Vale Hounds, followed by John Hamlin 1862-1875 and James Archer Swan

1875-1898. Mary Swan is listed as the landlady in 1902 but according to *The Castle Cary Visitor* the licence was transferred to Ann Charles Swan, the widow of James Swan, in 1899 and she is listed by 1906, leaving in 1913, Frederick Cave came in 1913 and in the following year the stables were demolished and the road junction widened. He left around 1918 followed by Arthur James Codling 1918-1930, and then William Henry Adams from 1931. Tom Moores in his recollections says that two men with this surname were the landlords. However the directories show that William's brother Sydney ran a business adjacent to the pub which probably accounts for the confusion. Stephen Barnard Viney is listed as the publican in 1939, Ernest and Mary Creed were here in 1957 and Harold and Muriel Galpin the following year. Raymond Victor Wilton was here briefly, having been the last licensee of the **Half Moon** when that closed in 1963. In more recent years it was run as a Chinese Restaurant but closed about 2006.

Weeks, Frederick
Recorded as a beerseller in South Cary in one directory in 1914

Wheatsheaf
On the corner of Smallway Lane in South Cary. It was opened probably between 1839 and 1841 as a beerhouse, although another note says it was built for Mr C C Wallis,[39] surgeon, about 1849 by E O Francis, a well-known local builder who was responsible for many of the houses in the town. Thomas Garland, who with his brother, had previously run a coal yard and hauliers business on the site, is the earliest recorded landlord from 1841 to 1857, followed by his widow who may be the Mary Garland listed as a beerseller in South Cary in 1861. The next recorded landlord is Charles Coleman 1866-1875 followed by James Carr and Joseph Chapman, then Charles Creed from 1886 until his death in 1912 and Elizabeth Creed up to 1923. Their son Alfred Frank Creed died in 1919 following war service. It was owned by Somerton Brewery by 1896 and their successors by 1925 when renewal of the licence was refused. By 1948 it was a house known as the Old Wheatsheaf.

Cornelius Martin refers to the **Savage Cat** in his memoirs of the late nineteenth century, published in the parish magazine and reprinted in *More Memories of Castle Cary and Ansford*, but does not say which public house this is. He does however name the licensee as Mr Coleman of Smallway and a note in *The Castle Cary Visitor* says this was indeed the nickname of the Wheatsheaf during the tenancy of Charles Coleman.

This inn was also known as **Beggars Bush.** This place name occurs quite frequently throughout the country and usually derives from a place, sometimes a tavern, often an actual tree or bush, where beggars would gather or shelter. The saying 'to go home by beggar's bush' meant to go to ruin. In this case the 1840 Tithe map shows it as the name of a field adjacent to the Wheatsheaf which was occupied in that year by the landlord Thomas Garland. It also harks back to the traditional use of a bush as a sign outside a house where drink may be had.[40]

White Hart

The White Hart in the 1930s during local road works

Fore Street. Inns called the White Hart were originally named from the badge of Richard II and they were once so common that for a while the name became virtually synonymous with tavern or inn. Prior to its use as an inn this building had been occupied by William Bulgin, a cabinet maker, possibly related to the carpenter John Bulgin who opened the **Golden Lion**.

The White Hart was opened, probably originally as a beerhouse, by John Marshall in 1836. An undated pencilled note in the 1841 tithe book says that John Marshall had a brewhouse on a garden located in the area that is now part of Millbrook. This may be the former brewhouse to the rear of Millbrook that was reported as damaged by fire in June 1906.

John was followed by his sons James and Thomas Marshall in 1846. Premises in the yard were destroyed by fire in 1848. John Marshall appears to be here again from 1850 until 1861, then William Purchase and George Henry Napper in 1866. Largely rebuilt or refronted in 1872 it was for a period the parcel office for the Somerset and Dorset Joint Railway.

George Hodges was here from 1872 until 1881, Arthur Jeffrey during the early 1880s, George Henry Kingston 1885 to 1906, James Weeks 1907 to 1927 and then Bessie Weeks. She was still living here in 1957 but the licensee was Herbert J Parham. Another of the local pubs eventually owned by Oakhill Brewery, by 1963 the licensees were John and

Margaret Crawford but two years later it was occupied by Peter and Pamela Aylott. Throughout the 1980s the pub was run by Charlie and Fiona Anderson before they moved to the **Britannia** in 1992. By 1997 the licensees were Steve and Rennie Wainwright.

White Horse

Montague House in Woodcock Street. Possibly open in the 1860s but not listed in the directories of the period and the only recorded landlord is James Rex in a note in *The Castle Cary Visitor*. This building subsequently became Lydford's builder's yard, then the veterinary surgery for many years, and is now a private house.

White Horse

In South Cary apparently on the land now occupied by Avalon and Ellesmere, a pair of semi-detached Edwardian villas. There are references in several manuscript lists. One is in the Living History Group files which states that the information is from; 'documents in the possession of Commander Sheppard of Avenue House.' Another is in the Museum archives and third is held by a local resident. The author cannot trace the documents belonging to Commander Sheppard and has been unable to find the source for the other lists. There do not appear to be any references to this public house in any printed record.

White, Stephen

Recorded as beerseller in South Cary 1852-1853. In 1852 during one of the several fires that occurred that year in South Cary his house was robbed of nearly £40.

White, Thomas *see* **Heart and Compass**

NOTES

1. The history of public houses and breweries, the relationship between the two and the licensing laws that governed their operation is an immensely complex subject. During most of the period under discussion it is a widely held belief that as well as considerable amounts of home brewing the majority of public houses brewed their own products, certainly well into the nineteenth century.

However brewing did exist as a separate industry dating back to the sixteenth century, indeed at that time it was the country's largest industry with many references to brewers in the legal records. The industry grew in the seventeenth century with the founding of large breweries in London and then later in other cities and towns. This led to the rise of the tied house system although this did not affect Castle Cary until late in the nineteenth century when some of the inns were bought by breweries based elsewhere.

2. William Macmillan (1844-1911) was from one of the families of Scottish drapers that migrated from Ayrshire in the early nineteenth century. Born in Wincanton but later taken to Birmingham he returned to Somerset in 1867. Joining John Boyd's horsehair business in Castle Cary as accountant and later secretary, he eventually took over the running of the company. Residing at Ochiltree House in Upper High Street he was very much involved in local affairs. His son Douglas (1884-1969) having encountered difficulty finding nursing help for his father during his final illness was then inspired to found the Macmillan Cancer Care Charity.

3. Other public house names that can be traced back to similar origins include; Catherine Wheel, named for an Egyptian Christian tortured on a wheel by the Romans; Cross Keys, the emblem of St Peter the gatekeeper of Heaven; Peter's Finger, the sign of benediction; and Salutation, the greeting of the Archangel Gabriel to Mary

4. Primarily intended for the temporary incarceration of drunkards and other miscreants, the **Castle Cary Round House** is one of the few surviving examples of a circular lock-up. Many others of various shapes, mainly square, rectangular and octagonal, can be found throughout the country and although some have been much altered or converted for other uses, a significant number are now listed buildings. They date mainly from the

eighteenth and nineteenth centuries although there are references to round houses as places of detention as early as 1589. Offenders would be locked up here until they sobered up or a magistrate was available to deal with them. Typically they have one door and may possibly have a small window high up in the wall hence the common name 'blind house', although they had other names in various places.

In Castle Cary the decision was taken in 1779 at a Vestry Meeting at the Angel Inn that there was a need of a temporary lockup. To cover the cost of building the funds of three small charities were appropriated and it was built on Bailey Hill 'where the tree stands.' According to the overseers accounts the final cost was £23. In 1785 when the Sunday School was established the Committee resolved that; 'if any children above the age of seven years are found in the streets, &c., breaking the Sabbath, they shall be taken up and locked in the Round House during school hours.'

No records exist to show how much use was made of the Round House and the story that on one bitter winter's night, during the Christmas festivities, an unfortunate prisoner froze to death may be apocryphal. It is also claimed that the last prisoner to be confined here made good his escape through the drain. Another popular story says that the domed roof was the inspiration for the shape of the police helmet.

Lock ups fell out of use after the County Police Act of 1839, which established proper police stations with holding cells, came into force. In Castle Cary the constable was housed in the Market House and two cells were inserted into the ground floor. With the Castle Cary Round House falling into disrepair it was eventually given to the town by the then lord of the manor, Sir Henry Hoare. Various repairs were undertaken and today it remains a quirky curiosity for visitors with the keys available for those who want to experience how incarceration felt. Recently it has been licensed as an unusual wedding venue.

Around the country there are over 150 surviving examples. Circular lock-ups are relatively uncommon, although not as rare as the plaque on the one in Castle Cary would suggest. This says that there are four in the country but recent research has so far revealed a total of eleven others. The others are located in Wiltshire at Shrewton, Everton on Merseyside, at Alton in Staffordshire, Harrold in Bedfordshire, Shenley in Hertfordshire, Digby in Lincolnshire, Breedon in Leicestershire, Pangbourne in Berkshire, Great Weldon in Northamptonshire, Holme upon Spalding Moor in Yorkshire and Barmouth in Gwynedd. This last one has two cells instead of the usual one, each with its own external door allowing the constable to lock up men and women separately.

5. Revd James Woodforde (1740-1803) led the life of a typical eighteenth-century clergyman. His claim to fame is the immensely detailed diary that he kept in a series of seventy-two notebooks from 1759 until 1802. Now published in their entirety by the Parson Woodforde Society they provide a detailed and valuable source of information relating to the social life of the period.

His father Samuel Woodforde (1695-1771) was the rector of Ansford and vicar of Castle Cary for many years, having been granted the living by Rachel Ettrick, the granddaughter of Anthony Ettrick who had bought the castle estate. James became his father's curate for some years and expected to succeed him. However on her death, Mrs Ettrick left her property to Anne Powell (1702-1775) her servant and companion. Mrs Powell sold the rectory to James Woodforde's uncle, Thomas Woodforde (1706-1796) who then installed his son Francis (1748-1836) as rector. This action precipitated James' move to Weston Longville in Norfolk where he spent the rest of his life as the vicar.

6. Edmund Rack (1735-1787) was born into a Quaker family in Attleborough in Norfolk. Trained as a dyer, he moved to Bath in 1775. Involved in advances in farming, he was among those who formed what became the Royal Bath and West of England Society and was its first secretary. He published volumes of poetry and essays and a life of William Penn. Needing to find additional income, he was employed by John Collinson to conduct a survey for use in the latter's history of Somerset. Now that an edited edition of Rack's work has been published it is seen to be a major contribution to the history of the county.

7. Carey Pearce Coombs (1842-1921) born in Frome, was the local doctor in Castle Cary for over forty years. He lived in Wason House and then moved across the road to Beechfield House (also known as The Villa or Cary Villa and now Cary Place). In 1866 he married Mary Leslie Franklin from Coventry and one of their sons, Carey Franklin Coombs (1879-1932) followed his father into medicine and became a widely respected cardiologist.

8. Henry Phelps (1817-1905) joined the Royal Navy in 1832 and served through a period that saw the start of the change from sailing ships to powered vessels. Serving in various ships he saw action in the Kaffir War of 1834, the storming of St Jean d'Acre in 1840, when he was flag-lieutenant to Sir Charles Napier, Kiang-Foo in 1842, the River Plate in 1847 and the Black Sea in 1854-56,. He was twice wounded and received the Syrian medal and Crimean and Turkish Medals. In 1849 he married Jane Wason Russ (1817-1898). He achieved the rank of captain in 1864 and retired in 1870, being promoted Rear-Admiral in 1900.

9. This is a reference to the various laws requiring people to swear allegiance to the monarch amid ongoing fears of a Catholic Jacobite rebellion during the early eighteenth century. Princess Sophia, Electress of Hanover (1630-1714), was the granddaughter of James I and became the next acceptable Protestant heir to the British throne when the last of Queen Anne's children died in 1701. In the event she just predeceased Anne and the throne passed to her son who succeeded as George I. In inns, when drinking the loyal toast, Jacobite sympathisers would surreptitiously hold their glass over the jug of beer thus saluting "the King over the water", that is, The Old Pretender or his son Bonnie Prince Charlie.

10. Claver Morris (1659-1727) was a West Country physician born in Caundle Bishop in Dorset who lived in Wells from 1686. He was well-read in science and the classics, a lover of social gatherings and a holder of public offices. An enthusiastic amateur musician, able to play several instruments, he was involved in the founding of the local music society. A heavily edited version of his diary was published in 1934 and extracts from his household accounts appear in several issues of '*Notes and Queries for Somerset and Dorset.*'

As well as many references to the inns in Wells, his diary gives an indication of the huge amounts of drink that even a relatively modest household would consume. He records brewing up to 7000 gallons of strong ale yearly and in addition he purchased substantial amounts of other drinks such as claret. This was often smuggled as he records one consignment being seized by the excise. Smuggling was rife at this period because of the high excise duty imposed on many commodities.

11. John Cannon (1684-ca1743) Born into a prosperous farming family in West Lydford he became an excise officer and wrote a lengthy memoir recently published as the '*Chronicles of John Cannon*'. In his work he travelled the area extensively and Castle Cary figures regularly in his book. He describes brewing and the assessment for duty locally and did some of his training in Castle Cary

12. Reginald Tucker (c 1725-1775) was convicted of one of the most notorious murders in the area. Born in Huish Episcopi and apprenticed to a bellows maker he absconded and joined the army until wounded at the Battle of Culloden. He came to Ansford and resumed his trade. He married in 1750 and moved to London for some years before returning having become rich in possibly dubious circumstances. In an argument about a meal he attacked and murdered his wife with a hammer.

His trial and execution were recorded in a pamphlet *"The Trial of Reginald Tucker for the wilful murder of Martha his Wife..."* which appears to be extremely rare with only one

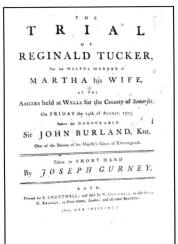

copy currently recorded. The family name is now recalled in Tuckers Lane in Ansford. Tucker's mother Elizabeth married for the third time in 1749 to Gaddis Jones.

13. It is now accepted that people were considerably more mobile in the past than previously believed, despite the poor state of most roads. Then the development of the turnpike roads during the eighteenth century brought about a revolution in transport so that by 1765, as well as an extensive system of public stage coaches, there were some 20,000 private coaches on the roads. As an eighteen year old tourist in England in 1784, the French aristocrat Francois de la Rochefoucauld commented 'You cannot imagine the quantity of travellers who are always on the road in England. You cannot go from one post to another without meeting two or three post chaises, to say nothing of the regular diligences.'

14. The elopement or abduction became a notorious case at the time and was widely reported in the newspapers. However it is only this entry in Woodforde's diary that allows us to make the link with the Perry family of the Ansford Inn.

Clementina Clarke inherited a huge fortune from her uncle who had estates in Jamaica. Richard Perry, a surgeon and apothecary in Bristol, managed by subterfuge to persuade her to elope with him to Gretna Green where they were married despite her age. They fled to the continent but returned over a year later and Perry was arrested. Imprisoned in some luxury with his young wife and her mother, their first child, a daughter, was born here.

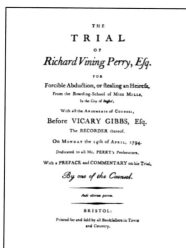

He finally came to trial in 1794 and after considerable argument Clementina was allowed to give evidence. Claiming that she was entirely happy with her situation Perry was immediately acquitted. Twin daughters were born later that year and a fourth daughter a few years later. It seems likely that after 1810 they had separated, Perry apparently living in Jamaica on the proceeds of the inheritance and Clementina reduced to begging in various towns including Bath where she died in 1813. Three of the daughters survived to receive part of the inheritance, although only one married and had children one of whom married into a landed family.

15. Reputedly haunted and named for a large drinking glass, the Rummer Tavern in All Saints Lane leading to the Flower Market has a long history. Known by this name for over two hundred years it became the first coaching inn in Bristol in 1784. It was the first drinking house in the city to be licenced and it can be traced back to at least 1241 when it was called The Greene Lattis. The use of a lattice to cover windows, more usually red in colour, was the sign of an alehouse.

The many changes of landlord at the Ansford Inn and in other public houses shows how common this practice was as each tried to better themselves and move to more prestigious establishments,

16. Revd John Skinner (1772-1839) also stopped in Castle Cary to visit his friend and fellow cleric Richard Warner who lived at nearby Ansford House in the 1820s. Born at Claverton, he worked originally as a lawyer before becoming vicar of Camerton in 1830. He was, like many clerics, a keen amateur antiquarian, involved in many archaeological digs and investigations in various sites around Somerset. He seems to have suffered from paranoia and eventually committed suicide. Extracts from his diary were published in 1930.

17. John Fry was the son of George Fry (1827-1906) who was the innkeeper at what was then called the New Inn on the A359 in nearby Galhampton, recently reopened as the Orchard Inn.

18. Live and Let Live. Pubs were given this name when the landlord thought there was some unfair competition occurring locally. This could be the opening of a rival inn, the imposition of new restrictions or taxes, or the opening of a railway that might take away trade. With the railway reaching Castle Cary in 1856 this seems the most likely reason.

19. John Bettey (1828-1883) is a typical example of the self-employed workers of the period who did various jobs including a spell as a publican or beerhouse keeper. Son of a yeoman farmer from near Martock he was first a farmer himself at East Lydford then by 1861 he is listed as a beerseller in Castle Cary, leaving in about 1866. By 1871 he was in Bristol where he was a labourer and in 1881 he was still a labourer but shown as out of work. He died two years later in Bristol.

20. Made mainly of copper or brass, tokens or checks were often issued by shops and other business including pubs during the nineteenth and early twentieth centuries. In pubs they were used to purchase drinks and are frequently found in connection with public house games. However there are very few references to them in contemporary literature and there is no precise explanation of how they were used. In Castle Cary examples are also recorded from The George, the Waggon and Horses and the White Hart.

21. The railway had only reached as far as Frome by 1852 hence Jane Carlyle's need to continue by coach. There were two that ran daily between Frome and Yeovil; the 'Prince of Wales' owned by Preedys and Shepherd and the 'Times' owned by Ridgeway, White and Dodimead, both of which stopped at the Britannia.

The allusion to Ireland refers to a Castle Cary in Donegal. Cary is common as a place name on its own and in combination with other elements. As well as Ireland there are Castle Carys in Lanarkshire, on the island of Guernsey and in both Torbay and the Tamar Valley in Devon.

22. John Rapson served twenty eight years as a policeman then, like many in his profession, in retirement he became a landlord in Charlton Musgrove. This was probably at the Red Lion although the only directory entry for him lists him simply as a beer retailer in 1914.

23. Probably the James Lintern who is also recorded as a publican in Wincanton at this period. He was at the Bear Inn there in 1791 and the Greyhound in 1803, the year in which he died.

24. Thomas Biss' younger brother Robert served in the First World War and is recorded on the Castle Cary War Memorial. He died in France aged 19 shortly before the end of the war, sadly as a result of 'friendly fire.'

25. The Castle was located at the foot of Lodge Hill to the east of the town and was probably built about 1130 probably replacing an earlier wooden structure. Rectangular and some 78 feet long made it one of the largest Norman keeps in the country with only three others being larger. A geophysics survey carried out in 2011 shows that the castle was similar to Castle Rising in Norfolk. However it was surprisingly short-lived. Besieged twice during the civil war between Stephen and Matilda it seems to have fallen into decay soon after 1153 and was possibly burnt. Replaced by a manor house nearby, the stonework was utilised elsewhere throughout the town. All that can now be seen are the extensive earthworks.

26. Anthony Ettrick (1622-1703) A lawyer and antiquary who lived at Holt Lodge, Bournemouth. He held a number of local government posts in that area and as a magistrate is best known for committing the Duke of Monmouth for trial after his defeat at the Battle of Sedgemoor in 1685. Notoriously eccentric, Ettrick fell out with the Church and swore 'never to be buried within the church or without it.' He later relented, but only partially, and obtained permission to be buried in the wall of Wimborne Minster. He prepared his tomb in advance, convinced he would die in 1693. In the event he survived a further ten years and the date had to be painted over.

27. The story of **Jack White's Gibbet** has been much embroidered in various publications, especially versions written for the stage. The facts were established by William and Douglas Macmillan and these are confirmed by the contemporary account in the recently published memoirs of John Cannon. In 1730 a man called Sutton, a shoemaker from Shaftesbury, was charged with taking a letter from there to Somerton. He called at the

Sun Inn in Wincanton to ask directions and Jack White offered to walk with him part of the way.

During the journey they fell to arguing over White's attempts to molest some women that they met and probably because both were drunk. Eventually in a rage White battered Sutton to death with a fence stake. Failing to hide the body properly White was soon arrested, tried, sentenced and executed near the scene of the murder where the Bratton Seymour road meets the Wincanton road. His body was then hung in an iron cage at the scene where it remained for many years, thus giving his name to the site.

28. This amount of stabling was fairly typical for such large inns. They would have supplied horses for several coaches, both public and private, each day and may also have offered stabling to other owners. As shown in the advert quoted here, at this period the George occupied much more land than now.

29. The Somerton Brewery, founded by Mr Kerrison, was owned by Thomas Templeman by 1840. Later it became Ord, Battiscome and Elwes, names which are in the deeds of the George. They closed in 1920 and the business was bought by Bruttons of Yeovil (later Brutton, Mitchell & Toms) who also bought the Britannia and the Half Moon. The brewery became part of Bass in 1960 and closed in 1965. The Yeovil site became shops and housing and the brewery malthouse site is now Tesco's car park.

30. The George is now the only building in Castle Cary to have a thatched roof. Thatch would have been very common at one time but during the late eighteenth and nineteenth centuries there was much rebuilding and alteration of the buildings in the town. As part of this most of the thatch was replaced by tile or slate. However at least one house in North Street still retains its thatch under the tiles where it now offers a good level of insulation.

31. *The Castle Cary Visitor* has two slightly different versions of this story. In the first the vicar is named as James Woodforde's cousin; Revd. Francis Woodforde (1747-1836) Rector of Ansford and also curate of Castle Cary for many years. The alternative version says it was Francis' son Thomas who at around this time became his successor as curate.

32. Thomas White (1825-1905) was from a family of blacksmiths who operated a forge near the Britannia. Thomas however, chose to become a carpenter and ran his business from Mill Lane. Much later he also became a director of John Boyd and Co. the horsehair weaving firm which still survives in the town. Eventually he retired to South Cary and sold the pub.

33. Bernard's son **Nathaniel John Bellringer** was the organist at St Andrew's Church in Ansford. He died aged 30 in March 1917 and there is a memorial plaque to him in the church

34. This was *The Somerset Visitor* another temperance magazine edited by William Macmillan which ran from 1879 until 1894 after which it was succeeded in 1896 by *The Castle Cary Visitor.* Although covering a somewhat wider area it is considerably less interesting than its successor, concentrating almost entirely on temperance meetings and with suitably uplifting and pious stories.

35. Jonathan Crocker (1744-1819) was an exact contemporary of Woodforde, who refers to him as 'Crocker the carrier' in one entry and in others mentions him in connection with supplying horses, acting as a pallbearer and singing in the church. Woodforde does not say he is a publican nor does *The Castle Cary Visitor*, which describes him as a prominent figure in local affairs, saying that he was a farmer and the tenant of Cockhill Farm, possibly as early as 1785, certainly until 1808 when it was advertised for sale. A history of the family, written by an Australian descendant, states that the family had been resident at this farm since the late seventeenth century.

Jonathan was a churchwarden at various times between 1778 and 1811 and in 1779 he was among those who agreed to build the round house lock-up on Bailey Hill. His father, also Jonathan, (1706-1762) was a churchwarden in the 1740s and also an overseer of the poor. In this latter capacity he was one of signatories of letters addressed to the magistrates in 1744 calling for the closure of alehouses in Castle Cary (see page 9)

36. No further information about Mr Nevil or his machine has been found. It clearly related to the weaving of woollen cloth but by this period the trade was already undergoing major changes in some areas, with linen taking over because of the availability of flax. However, within a few years the linen trade also collapsed when cheap imports appeared, in Castle Cary to be replaced with sailcloth and twine manufacture and later also horsehair cloth weaving. Boyd's, the last remaining factory producing this material, survives in Castle Cary.

37. The Independent Order of Rechabites, a friendly society founded in 1835 as part of the Temperance Movement and connected with the Methodist Church. Of necessity involved in monetary matters it eventually evolved into a financial institution which still exists.

38. One local guidebook published in 1999 says that this building was a temperance hotel. However as Hoskins' was only ever a coffee house the author suspects that the writer is confusing the two establishments discussed here.

39. Charles Cornwallis Wallis (1798-1877) was a surgeon in Castle Cary for many years. With his wife Sarah Catherine (nee Watts) he lived in the house built on the original market house site in the centre of Castle Cary. This he subsequently demolished and sold the land to the company that built the current Market House in 1855. He moved to the High Street to a house on the site later occupied by Stuckey's Bank and its successors.

40. There is a very bizarre explanation of the name Beggars Bush made by the Bishop of Clifton, writing in the *Somerset Archaeological Proceedings* of 1875. He writes that it is a corruption of beckers-huish, the hostelry of the beckers, the men who had charge of the beacons. However this etymology is very fanciful and is certainly not recognised by the *Oxford English Dictionary* which does not include the word becker.

BIBLIOGRAPHY

Primary Sources:
Documents
Ansford Tithe map and Apportionment Book, 1838
Ansford, St Andrews Church, parish register transcripts
Castle Cary and Ansford, Census returns 1841-1911, National Archives, HO 107, RG 9-14,
Castle Cary Tithe map and Apportionment book, 1840/1
Castle Cary, All Saints Church, parish register transcripts
Deeds and other documents relating to various individual properties in The Somerset Heritage Centre, Castle Cary Museum and private collections.

Books
Cannon, John. *Chronicles of John Cannon, Excise Officer and Writing Master, 1684-1743*, ed John Money, British Academy, 2010
Clarke, Robert. *Memoirs of Robert Clarke of Castle Cary*, Compton & Ritchie, 1829
Dunion, Patrick. *Castle Cary from Old Photographs*. Fox Publications 1983
Grafton, Revd A W. *Historical Notes on Castle Cary*, Bentley, [ca 1890]
Hershon, Cyril P. *The Castles of Cary*, Pavalas Press Bristol, 1990
Langmaid, Nancy. *Castle Cary to Durston, the story of a railway*, Railway Centenary 2006
Lush, B & Carter, J (eds.) *Castle Cary War Memorial*, Living History Group, 2014
McGarvie, Michael. *Castle Cary; a sketch of its industrial and social history with special reference to Boyd's Hair Factory*, Avalon Industries, 1980
Miller, S & Laver B (eds.) *Castle Cary, North Cadbury and Wincanton*, Chalford, 1997
Pearse A (ed.) *Castle Cary and Ansford; Time to Reflect*, Living History Group, 2002
Pearse A (ed.) *Memories of Castle Cary and Ansford*, Living History Group, 1998
Pearse A (ed.) *More Memories of Castle Cary and Ansford*, Living History Group, 2012
Rack, Edmond. *Rack's Survey of Somerset*, ed. M McDermott, & S Berry, SANHS, 2011
Richardson, Miranda. *An Archaeological Assessment of Castle Cary*, English Heritage & Somerset County Council, 2003
Siraut, Mary, (ed.) *Victoria County History of Somerset, Vol X; Castle Cary & the Brue-Cary Watershed*, Boydell & Brewer, 2010
Woodforde, Revd James. *The Diary of a Country Parson, 1758-1802*, ed. J Beresford, 5 volumes, OUP 1924-31
Woodforde, Revd James. *The Diary of James Woodforde 1759-1802* ed. R L Winstanley et al, 17 volumes, The Parson Woodforde Society, 1979-2014.

Periodicals
The Castle Cary Visitor, ed William Macmillan et al 1896-1915
Parson Woodforde Society, Quarterly Journal, ed R L Winstanley et al. Vol 1, 1968 et seq,
The Somerset Visitor, ed. William Macmillan, 1879-1894
The Visitor (originally called *The New Visitor*) ed P & H Dunion, 1983 et seq

Directories

Bragg, William. *General Directory of the County of Somerset*, 1840

Harrison, Harrod & Co. *Bristol Post Office Directory and Gazetteer...and Somersetshire*, 1830

Hunt & Co. *Directory of Dorsetshire...and...Castle Cary*, 1851

Kelly & Co. *Directory of Somerset*, 1866, 1883, 1889, 1894, 1897, 1902, 1906, 1910, 1914, 1919, 1923, 1927, 1931, 1935, 1939

Kelly, E R (ed.) *Post Office Directory of Somerset*, 1859, 1861, 1875

Morris & C. *Directory and Gazetteer of Somerset*, 1872

Pigot & Co. *National Commercial Directory.....*, 1830,

Pigot & Co. *Directory and Topography...*, 1834

Robson, William, *Universal British Directory*, 1793-8

Robson, William. *Commercial Directory of London and the Western Counties* [1840]

Slater & Co. *National and Commercial Directory...of...Somerset*, 1852-3

Smith & Co. *Bath and Somerset Directory* 1865-6

Secondary Sources

Anon. *The Trial of Richard Vining Perry, Esq for forcible abduction....*Bristol [1794]

Bates, E H (ed). *Quarter Sessions Records for the County of Somerset, Vol 1 James I, 1607-1625*, Somerset Record Society, 1907

Bates, E H (ed). *Quarter Sessions Records for the County of Somerset, Vol 2 Charles I, 1625-1639* Somerset Record Society, 1908

Bates-Harbin, E H (ed). *Quarter Sessions Records for the County of Somerset, Vol 3, Commonwealth 1646-1660*, Somerset Record Society, 1912

Brooke, Leslie. *Some West-Country Lock-Ups, in the counties of Somerset, Dorset, Avon, Wiltshire, Devon & Cornwall*, Fox Publications, Castle Cary, 1985

Brown, Reid Frederick. *Abstracts of Somerset Wills, Fifth Series*, F A Crisp, 1890

Carlyle, Thomas & Carlyle, Jane Welsh, *Selected Letters Vol 27 1852*, ed K Fielding, et al, Duke University, Durham NC, 1999

Collinson, Revd. John. *The History and Antiquities of the County of Somerset*, 1791, facsimile reprint, Allan Sutton, 1983

Dawes, M C B (ed). *Quarter Sessions Records for the County of Somerset, Vol 4, Charles II, 1666-1677*, Somerset Record Society, 1919

Dobbie, B M Willmott. *Pounds or Pinfolds and Lockups, Beast and Man in Custody*, Bath University Library, 1979

Duck, Sandra. *Crocker Chronicles, 1670-1999*, Launceston, Tasmania, 1999

Dunkley, Leslie & Wright, Gordon. *Dictionary of Pub Names*, Routledge, 1987

Eason, Helena. *Bristol's Historic Inns*, Redcliffe Press, 1982

Everitt, Alan. *Landscape and Community in England*, Hambledon Press, 1985

Fowler, Simon. *Researching Brewery & Publican Ancestors*, Family History Partnership, 2009

Gass, D[avid] *The Days that Were, a short history of Zion Chapel*, Castle Cary, 1943

Gibson, Jeremy. *Victuallers' Licences, Records for Family and Local Historians*, 3rd edn. Family History Partnership, 2009

Haydon, Peter. *Beer and Britannia; an Inebriated History of Britain*, Sutton Publishing, 2001

Hey, David, (ed.) *Oxford Companion to Local and Family History*, OUP, 1998

Hopkins, Mary Alden. *Hannah More and Her Circle*, Longman Green, 1947

Jennings, Paul. *The Local; A History of the English Pub*, Tempus Publishing, 2007

Kain. Roger & Prince, Hugh. *The Tithe Surveys of England and Wales*, CUP 1885

Latimer, John. *Annals of Bristol in the Eighteenth Century*, Bristol 1893

Macmillan, Douglas. *Jack White's Gibbet, the Fiction and the Facts*, Somerset Folk Press, 1922

Macmillan, Douglas. *The Round House in Castle Cary*, Somerset Folk Press, 1922

Mathias, Peter. *The First Industrial Nation, an economic history of Britain*, 1700-1914, 2nd edn, Methuen, 1983

Miller, S. *The Parson's Quarter Companion*, Castle Cary, 1997

Miller, S. *From Parson's Quarter to Purgatory, a history of North Cadbury, Galhampton and Woolston*, Castle Cary, 1988

Minnit, S C et al. *Somerset Public House Tokens*, Somerset County Council, 1985

Morris, Claver. *The Diary of a West Country Physician, AD 1684-1726*, ed. E Hobhouse, Simpkin Marshall, 1934

Popham, Hugh. *The Somerset Light Infantry*, Hamish Hamilton, 1968

Porter, G R. *The Progress of the Nation…from the beginning of the nineteenth century*, John Murray, 1847

Saunders, Philip T. *Stuckey's Bank*, Taunton, Barnicott & Pearce, 1928

Skeggs, James. *Somerset Inn Signs*, The Author, Wellington, 2004

Skinner, John. *Journal of a Somerset Rector, 1803-1834*, ed H & P Coombs, rev edn, Kingsmead, 1971

Smith, G Munro. *History of Bristol Royal Infirmary*, Bristol, 1917

Sweetman, George. *The History of Wincanton, Somerset, from the Earliest Times to the year 1903*, Wincanton, 1903

Websites

www.castlecaryansfordlivinghistory.org.uk/
Castle Cary and Ansford Living History Group. Our local history group
www.pubhistorysociety.co.uk
http://pubshistory.com
www.deadpubssociety.org.uk
Sites with background detail and references to Somerset pubs.
www.yeovilhistory.info A mine of information about Yeovil with a pubs section that has material on licensing and other related topics.

INDEX

Main entries are shown in bold